They
Call Him The
Walking Bible

They
Call Him The
Walking Bible

By
ROGER F. CAMPBELL

Nashville / New York

Second printing

Copyright © 1977 Jack Van Impe Crusades

JACK VAN IMPE CRUSADES

Box J Royal Oak, Michigan 48068

ISBN 0-8407-9000-7

Author's Introduction

I first met Jack and Rexella Van Impe more than twenty years ago when they came to my church to conduct a crusade. They stayed in our home and were quickly taken to our hearts. Their Christian conduct convinced me they were genuine.

Since that time, I have worked closely with them on a number of occasions, twice in large united crusades in the area where I was a pastor.

In more recent years, I have been a pastor not far from their international headquarters. A number of the members of my congregation have worked in their offices. I have had ample opportunity to observe their ministry and to know their reputation here. As a result, my first evaluation still stands. They are genuine.

I am pleased to have the opportunity of presenting the life-story of "The Walking Bible." It is a fitting title for a man who has so immersed himself in the Word of God.

I will be especially pleased if the work of God in the life of Dr. Jack Van Impe is found clear enough in these pages to bring many readers to full commitment to Jesus Christ.

Roger F. Campbell
WATERFORD, MICHIGAN

To my Wife
whose love, respect, loyalty,
patience and encouragement
helped me establish and achieve
spiritual goals
God laid upon my heart.

. . . . DR. JACK VAN IMPE

Table of Contents

They
Call Him The
Walking Bible

Dr. and Mrs. Van Impe

CHAPTER ONE

A Voice Heard Around the World

It is the final night of the crusade, the culmination of months of planning and prayer. The crowd is arriving and the chatter of voices provides cover for the choir to rehearse its selection one more time. Those who have found their places early in order to enjoy the preliminary music strain to hear over the scuffing of feet and the buzz of conversation all around them.

In rooms beneath the stadium bleachers there is another kind of conversation going on as hundreds pray for this closing service. They are the counsellors, pastors, committee people, and others who have given of themselves to make all this happen.

Some who are making their way down the crowded aisles searching for seats will never forget this week. Their lives have been changed. They feel as if they have come to the end of a long search. Others are still searching.

A man escorts his wife down the stairs and to the row of chairs nearest the speaker's platform. They have decided to make one last try before divorce. It will be their night.

A teenage boy clutching a new Bible moves up the steps to the top row in the stadium.

Ushers assist an older gentleman in a wheelchair. He has been bitter about life since the accident that caused his paralysis. He had been on his way to a dance, hoping for some vicarious enjoyment in seeing others move about so freely, when the stadium sign attracted his attention and caused him to have his driver bring him to hear "The Walking Bible."

As the pastors and workers emerge from the prayer rooms, there is a quieting of the crowd. Eyes follow Dr. Van Impe and Rexella, his wife, as they join others who have platform responsibilities in this crusade finale.

Tonight's message will be prophetic, and everything in the service builds toward it. There is an expectant air in the crowd. They have been looking forward all week to this explanation of Bible prophecy as it relates to world events. Many have brought friends and relatives whose curiosity has been aroused by the timely topic.

First nighters eye the evangelist as the service develops. They see a man who has a burden, yet is human enough for a quick smile. He seems both distant and approachable. Immersed in thought, yet alert to everything around him.

Dr. Van Impe's part in the musical portion of the meeting provides many in the audience their first opportunity to hear the accorgan, an instrument that blends the benefits of both the accordion and the organ. His ability as a musician is established quickly. He is totally involved. A perfectionist.

The bond between this husband-wife team is too strong to be hidden. While Rexella is communicating with the crowd in testimony and song, the man in her life beams approval. And well he might. He knows her ministry in music is no performance, and he respects the work of God through this lady so loved by crusade congregations around the world.

When the evangelist rises to preach there are mixed feelings throughout the stadium. There is anticipation of hearing the awaited prophetic message, but it is accompanied by a touch of sadness at this being the last message Dr. Van Impe will deliver to this audience.

Regular attenders are not surprised at the army of Bible verses marshalled to explain and prove each point of the sermon; they've come to expect it. Many feel as if they have been bathed in the Bible during these meetings, and the cleansing effect is showing in their lives. Old wrongs have been made right. Bills paid. Questionable practices dropped. Dedication renewed.

Newcomers are overwhelmed by the avalanche of inspiration. They have never heard this much Bible in so short a time. They are amazed at the evangelist's ability to quote the written Word of God. It is evident that his aim is to place his own personality in the background and to confront his hearers with an ultimatum from the Almighty. He seems to desire to be only a voice, forcing his audience to grapple with the Word.

In this setting and atmosphere the results are predictable. Conviction grows. Sin seems more sinful. The cross and resurrection appear in their proper Biblical perspective. Conversions take place. Backsliders return. The faithful are refueled. The fire spreads.

If this sacred stadium scene told the entire story, this alone would be worth telling. But there is much more. Modern media has made it possible for the Van Impe ministry to be multiplied around the world. That stream of searching people which moves forward at the close of the crusade is only the local portion of a world-wide harvest in which the Van Impes labor.

In an Indiana reformatory twenty prisoners gather around a radio weekly to hear Dr. Van Impe's broadcast. The walls these men have built within themselves inflict greater isolation than the barriers around their prison, but both are penetrated by Van Impe's radio ministry.

An agnostic was awakened at 7:30 a.m. by the voice of a preacher. He had turned on his radio the night before, thinking the soft music would help him sleep through the night. Captured by the events of prophecy being unfolded by Dr. Van Impe, he made a note of the time so he would not miss the broadcast the next week. Following that second broadcast he sought out his guitar teacher—a Christian—and arranged to attend church with him the following Sunday. That visit to church brought about his salvation. He is now earnestly trying to lead his devil-worshipping cousin to Christ.

A nurse in the Bahamas, West Indies, listens regularly to Radio Bonaire, one of the most powerful radio stations in the world. It was while listening to the Jack Van Impe Crusades broadcast, on that station, that she felt the tug of the Holy Spirit in her heart. She couldn't wait until the radio message was finished, but opened her life to Christ at that very moment. She is determined to spend the rest of her life winning souls and being a witness in her profession.

A Christian woman in Ghana, Africa, heard Dr. Van Impe bring a series of radio messages on soul winning. She became so convicted about her lack of concern for souls that she has influenced a number of her Christian friends to join her in regular witnessing.

In Wichita, Kansas, the Van Impe broadcast is carried on station KLEO. Recently, members of the station staff were surprised by the news that one of their disc jockeys had been converted. This fellow employee had been running Dr. Van Impe's broadcast regularly for several weeks. One morning he became so moved by the message that he fell to his knees and received Christ as his personal Saviour.

World-wide broadcasting has created an immense appetite for literature and recordings. From around the world the requests come; from Finland, Ceylon, New Zealand, South Africa, Australia, Ireland, and the list goes on. While varied in content, all letters have one thing in common; they represent people who have been touched by the ministry of "The Walking Bible."

One can only guess the impact of the thousands of booklets and recordings sent to distant places, but some reports find their way back to the crusade headquarters in Clawson, Michigan. One of the most moving is the account of the revival aboard the U.S.S. Forrestal while the ship was on a cruise in the Mediterranean.

Dr. Van Impe's booklet, "The Deadliest Sin," seems to have been the spark that ignited the faithful on the Forrestal. Christian sailors who were sharing the booklet became convicted about their indifference to the needs of lost people about them. After that, radio, recordings, and literature were all part of the divine program to bring revival to hundreds of American Navy men.

There were forty-five hundred men on board, and by the time the number of Christian sailors had reached one hundred they had made a covenant to witness to the entire crew.

This move of God soon began to bear all the marks of an old-fashioned revival. Prayer groups were formed. There was a decided difference in the men's lives. A commander wrote that his men were leading "Spirit-filled lives." Participants in the revival were willing to bear any kind of ridicule or reproach for the Lord's sake. Recordings of Dr. Van Impe's sermons were shared widely so that small congregations were gathered for preaching at every opportunity.

A genuine revival always produces conversions and the awakening on board the Forrestal was no exception. One sailor observed that ". . . scores are turning to Christ." Later, another reported that the number of converts had reached six hundred, and that the Forrestal fire had spread to the U.S.S. John F. Kennedy.

Television is the most recent challenge to be accepted by the Jack Van Impe Crusades. The decision was reached after much consideration and prayer. Aware of the great financial and physical resources demanded by extensive television ministry, Dr. Van Impe has stepped through this door cautiously. Those who know him, however, understand that once a commitment is made, his caution gives way to boundless energy and spiritual power. Response from initial telecasts has been well beyond expectations.

The discipline and drive that has enabled him to memorize more than eight thousand Bible verses will now be harnessed to present the Word of God in America's living rooms. It may be that one of the most significant events in America's bicentennial year will be the beginning of her television confrontation with the Bible through the voice of an evangelist named Jack Van Impe.

The growth and outreach of the Van Impe ministry has been

phenomenal. In a few years it has grown from single church crusades to a work that encircles the globe. The momentum is miraculous.

Why?

What goes into the building of a man who becomes a voice for God around the world? That is a question worth asking. And its answer is our quest in this look at the life of the man they call "The Walking Bible."

CHAPTER TWO

A Boy And A Book

Jack Van Impe was born in Freeport, Michigan on Feb. 9, 1931. He would be the only child of Oscar and Louise Van Impe to reach maturity, and would make their name known on every continent.

These young immigrant parents had left their home in Flanders, Belgium, in October of 1929, just two weeks after their wedding day, on a honeymoon trip to America. Their minds were filled with thoughts of love and money.

The plan was to work here until they had saved enough to return to their homeland and make a good start in life. Oscar's father, Joseph Van Impe, had taken this route in 1921 and after eight months of work in America had earned enough to purchase a fine home in Belgium. It was a good plan, but it was the most difficult time of the century to make it work. Their arrival here was almost simultaneous with the stock market crash that brought the Great Depression.

Detroit, Michigan, became home for the Van Impes that first winter. Conditions were bleak and difficult. Jobs were almost non-existent. The land of promise had become the land of problems. The money tree was barren. Bewildered but still hopeful, the newlyweds survived that first winter by living with relatives and stretching the nine dollars weekly paycheck that Louise earned at a pickle factory. Oscar was unemployed.

News of jobs in the sugar beet and vegetable fields of western Michigan lured Oscar and Louise out of the Motor City in the spring of 1930. Oscar ventured forth first with a crew of men recruited for this back-breaking labor, and Louise followed after housing was arranged for her.

It was a long hard summer. Evenings found them tired and frustrated. Something had gone wrong with their plan. Flanders beckoned, but they did not have the money to return. There seemed to be nothing to do but to keep moving down those long rows of pickles, beans, and sugar beets.

By mid-summer, the Van Impes had moved to Freeport. It was a small town surrounded by huge pickle farms. A few miles away lay the sugar beet fields. An old house was provided there for them by a farmer for whom they worked. Though hardly a newlywed's dream, Louise made it homey and when the harvest ended they decided to stay for the winter. They were expecting their first child. It had been a long journey from Flanders to Freeport.

No one knows who provided Oscar and Louise with their first Bible. They found it in the house for transient farm workers that had become their home. Whether some pious previous picker had left it by mistake or design cannot be told. Louise says she didn't know it was a Bible. That was fortunate, since both she and her husband had been taught in their youth that the Bible was a bad book—one that would, according to Oscar, "make you crazy."

The book was added to the couple's few possessions. It would travel with them for many years and its message would ultimately revolutionize their lives.

Winter in Michigan's vegetable country was even more frustrating than the hot busy summer. There was little to do but wait for spring. Income ended. In an effort to survive, the Van Impes developed their Freeport farmhouse into a base for bootlegging.

Oscar says he manufactured his moonshine in an old copper boiler, the top of which he sealed with bread dough to prevent steam from escaping. A tube coiled out of the top of the boiler, ran through cold water, and steadily dropped booze in a barrel. His Model-T-Ford, topless from an encounter with a tornado, became the delivery wagon, carrying whiskey to towns and villages around Freeport.

Meanwhile, back at the retail outlet (the old farmhouse), homemade beer was moving at ten cents a glass. Business was booming because the customers enjoyed Oscar's lively accordion music as a background for their drinking. It was better than beet picking for both income and excitement. There was one problem: those were prohibition days and it was against the law.

Fortunately, the Van Impe energy was not long to be invested in crime. A few of Oscar's Belgian buddies were arrested for bootlegging and sentenced to three years in prison. That was enough for Oscar. He closed his basement brewery and bar and settled back to await the birth of their first child.

February 9 was long in coming. Oscar was eager to see their firstborn and Louise was weary in waiting. When the moment finally arrived, however, their eagerness turned to anxiety. The birth was difficult and the young mother's life was in jeopardy.

She started her labor on Saturday and did not give birth until Monday. That weekend was filled with long, agonizing hours. It seemed doubtful that either Louise or the baby would come through alive.

It would be impossible to adequately describe Oscar's thoughts as he paced the floor of the old house that had now become hospital and delivery room. Questions haunted him: Why had he come to America? Had his young wife's work in the fields caused her complications? Should he have arranged for her to go to the hospital for delivery of their child? He tried praying but God seemed far away. He nearly despaired.

Finally the crisis was over. The cloud of concern lifted; Louise would live. She and Oscar looked into the face of their newborn son, and they named him Jack Leo Van Impe.

The newest member of the family was loved and wanted from the beginning. That bond of parental devotion has never wavered. Even during the turbulent years when alcohol influenced their home, Jack knew his parents cared. In those early years he was constantly the object of their affection and attention. He was the one part of their European dream that had come true.

It was quickly evident that baby Jack had a good set of lungs. While that is good equipment for worldwide preaching, his parents soon became disturbed with his "strong crying and tears." They discussed it with friends and finally concluded that the child was not getting enough to eat. He needed something more substantial than his bottle.

Acting on this advice, Oscar and Louise purchased oatmeal for their squalling offspring. They could hardly wait to see the promised effect. At last they would have a night of rest.

Following the directions of the kindly Quaker on the box, they prepared the cereal and poured it into the baby's bottle. (No one had told them to buy baby cereal or to feed the youngster with a spoon.)

The oatmeal, of course, refused to pass through the nipple and little Jack became more frustrated than ever. Seeing the problem, Oscar seized a pair of scissors and cut off the end of the nipple. The oatmeal rushed out so fast that the poor child nearly choked to death, frightening his parents sufficiently to keep him off the oatmeal diet until he was old enough to handle it.

The summer of 1931 was another season of hot grueling labor. The young mother worked with her husband in the fields while the baby waited, not far away, in an old buggy. This summer, however, the presence of that new life in the household made their existence more bearable. On pleasant Michigan summer evenings Oscar and Louise found diversion from the daily grind by watching signs of growth and development in their young son. They enjoyed one another and dreamed together.

Freeport remained their home until the spring of 1932, when they moved to Leipsic, Ohio. There they would experience their first real encounter with sorrow and meet a man who would have a part in changing their lives.

CHAPTER THREE

Life In Leipsic

Sugar beet growing in western Michigan had been an agricultural experiment. The results were disappointing and by 1932 many farmers had decided to plow their beet fields and return to the grain and dairy production for which they had been known in the past.

Unemployment loomed again.

Remembering that friends had left the Michigan beet fields for Ohio, the Van Impes contacted them and inquired about work there. The result was an invitation to a job and housing in Leipsic, Ohio.

Oscar and Louise loaded their possessions in the Model-T and began the long journey to another new home. Oscar had converted his once topless car into a pick-up truck by building a roof over the front seat and leaving the rear open for hauling. It was a typical depression-era moving van.

The faithful old Ford was taxed to the limit with their belongings. Besides Oscar and Louise, it contained furniture, crocks, wicker baskets of dishes, clothing, bedding, pots and pans, beer bottles, five gallons of whiskey, five rabbits, a book, and a boy. Departing from Freeport at 5 a.m. they arrived in Leipsic at 9 p.m. Oscar changed or repaired nine flat tires on that trip. It was a tired trio that settled down for the night in their new home in Ohio.

The house in Leipsic was quite comfortable and surrounded by neighbors. It was a community of sugar beet workers. They were friendly and helpful. The only unpleasant feature was a busy railroad that carried speeding trains within a few feet of the house several times each day. That hazard brought Oscar and Louise to the brink of the greatest potential tragedy of their lives.

Jack was just over one year old—still a creeper. He was at that dangerous age when it was easy to forget a child's ability to get around. That may have contributed to his escape one day from the otherwise watchful eye of his mother. Whatever the reason, young Jack found his way to the railroad tracks and sat down on them.

It was a shout from an alert neighbor who lived across the street that startled both Oscar and Louise and awakened them to the awful danger. They saw the man running at full speed toward the tracks; as their eyes followed him their hearts nearly stopped. There in the path of an oncoming train sat their only son.

Only eternity will reveal the importance of that rescue. There is no record that the newspapers carried the story of the neighbor's heroism. Even Oscar and Louise have forgotten the man's name. Yet millions hear the Word of God through the lips and life of the man who, as a boy, was lifted from the path of that speeding train by an unknown man who cared.

Was the devil trying to cut short a life that would one day be so used of God? Did the Holy Spirit turn the eyes of the neighbor to that track? Was this moving experience a part of God's early dealing with Jack's parents? What an interesting day it will be when God unfolds the mysteries of life to His own!

Life in Leipsic was much like it had been in Freeport. The rows of sugar beets were just as long, the sun equally hot, and the weeds as stubborn. Still, it was work. A means of livelihood. And in 1932, those were things coveted by many.

Jack was growing. Walking and talking. Each day seemed to bring more awareness of his tiny world, and his parents enjoyed each new discovery. They talked often of his future and envisioned it far from the sugar beet fields.

With money scarce, Jack's toys were few. Searching for

something to entertain her energetic youngster, Louise gave him the book she had found in the house at Freeport. It became his constant companion. He carried it, chewed on its pages, and slept with it. That old Bible seemed always to be with him.

Though unaware of the significance of her act, Louise had handed her son the book that would become his very life. In maturity, he would keep chewing its truth and digesting its wisdom. It would remain his favorite book, and the spreading of its message would become the consuming passion of his soul.

It was in Leipsic that the Van Impes met Pastor Ross, an assistant pastor in a Methodist church near their home. During visitation in the community one day he stopped to get acquainted. Oscar was delighted and asked Louise to bring their caller a bottle of beer. Pastor Ross declined the drink stating that he was a Christian.

That rattled Oscar. He considered himself a Christian. A good one. But that didn't interfere with his drinking. He concluded there must be something wrong with this fellow and was glad when he left.

Pastor Ross, however, was determined to develop a friendship with his new prospects. He was faithful in his witness about Christ and seemed undaunted even though they gave no evidence of being interested in his message. Grudgingly, Oscar began to build respect for this short, persistent Scotsman.

When winter arrived, another child was expected. Oscar and Louise were torn between excitement and apprehension. They liked the thought of a playmate for Jack, but remembered the difficult birth and feared a repeat of the experience.

The months of waiting were uneasy ones, especially for Oscar. He kept reliving that waiting time at Jack's birth and sometimes blamed himself for placing Louise's life in danger. He increased his drinking a bit to rid himself of tensions.

Besides, it helped keep his mind off his financial frustrations. The fortune he had expected when leaving Flanders seemed to have been but a wasted dream. He wondered how long he would be on this treadmill lined with rows and rows of sugar beets.

When Charlotte Van Impe was born that July morning in

1933, her parents were delighted. The birth had brought complications, as they had feared, but both mother and child had survived. Their joy was brief, however; their daughter lived but two hours.

Oscar and Louise were heartbroken at their loss. No relatives were present to share their grief and had it not been for Pastor Ross they would have felt completely forsaken.

But that faithful man was there. Praying. Counselling. Comforting. Speaking about Charlotte being in heaven at that very moment.

Immersed in their sorrow, these young mourners hardly knew how to react to assurances that were so different from their ideas about life and death. Nevertheless, they were grateful for someone who cared.

Funeral arrangements were blocked because Oscar did not have the money to care for a proper burial. He could afford neither priest nor plot. But, once again, Pastor Ross was available. He bought the casket, arranged for the burial, and brought words of comfort when they left young Charlotte's tiny body in the cemetery at Leipsic. The Van Impes would never forget his kindness even though they did not, at that time, receive his Lord.

Shortly after Charlotte's death it was decided that Jack should be baptized in the Roman Catholic Church. While not regular attenders, that had been their religious affiliation in Flanders and on a few occasions they had gone to church in America. Godparents were chosen and the act carried out in a church near their home. Jack was not quite three years old at his baptism.

Unaware that a move was so near at hand, Oscar and Louise spent Christmas in 1933 with the usual European festivities. There were a few toys for Jack and they enjoyed his wide-eyed excitement. Booze flowed freely. Somehow there always seemed to be money for that. Besides, it was customary. It was the accepted way to celebrate the birth of Christ.

The usual post-holiday letdown moved in, making the invitation of friends to visit Detroit all the more attractive. They accepted and set out on a trip that ended their sugar beet labor forever. Oscar found work at the Plymouth Motor Car Company, and the Detroit area has remained their home to this day.

Louise Van Impe and Jack at 1½ years.

Oscar Van Impe and Jack at 5 years.

CHAPTER FOUR

The Music Man

With his family comfortably settled in a small house on the East Side of Detroit, Oscar reflected on the combination of events that had brought them out of the beet fields and back to the city that had been their first home in America.

What had seemed to be just an enjoyable visit with friends in Detroit had turned up an opportunity for employment in an automobile plant. The very thought of escaping that short-handled beet hoe (a real backbreaker) had sent him hurrying to the long job line outside the Plymouth Motor Car Company.

His first day of waiting was in vain. All applicants who had not been formor employees were sent home. Feeling he had learned his lesson, Oscar returned the next day and told the employment officials that he had worked there previously. As a result, he was immediately ushered into the employment office. There, a file folder was pulled on Oscar Van Impe and the men who were doing the hiring looked on in disbelief. The file belonged to Oscar's uncle who was twenty-five years older than the man who now stood before them.

Frightened, Oscar confessed all, fully expecting to be arrested for attempting to defraud the company. To his surprise, however, he was hired on the spot and put to work that very day. It was a pivotal experience in his life, one that would ultimately cause him to meet the man who would lead him to Christ.

The job in the factory was steady work. The wage was sixty-three cents an hour and, for the first time since arriving in America, Oscar could count on a paycheck the year around. The Van Impes began to feel their American dream might become a reality after all.

Oscar Van Impe is a man of intense energy and drive. It seems to be a family trait. That characteristic, coupled with his experience of working long hours in the beet fields, made him restless at the end of the day and on weekends. He felt as if he was wasting time that could somehow be used to increase his income, and he began to look for opportunities for more work and challenge.

Remembering his success with the accordion in his short-lived bootlegging venture, Oscar began to think about putting his musical ability to work in the beer gardens and night clubs that dotted the Belgian sector of Detroit. He had begun playing at the age of seventeen and had taken to it naturally. Now he saw this talent as a means of added income and decided to pursue the idea.

A letter to his father expressing his desire for a good instrument brought a gift from Belgium of ten thousand francs ($200.00). Adding that to his savings, Oscar ordered a new chromatic accordion. It was a "Universal," built to his personal specifications, covered with pearl and encrusted with jewel-like stones. His name appeared in bold letters on its front so he would be remembered by those he entertained. When the accordion arrived, the music man was ready for business.

And business came.

The Belgian beer gardens opened to Oscar as if they had been waiting for him. He played his way into Belgian hearts and became a favorite for picnics, parties, weddings, and night clubs. Every weekend found Oscar entertaining until the early hours of the morning. The pay was good, by depression standards, and he was excited about his new "extra" occupation.

The entertainment business sometimes divides families. Fortunately, that didn't happen to the Van Impes. Louise accompanied Oscar on the tavern circuit and took young Jack along to be entertained by the beer hall customers. He soon became a favorite of the drinking crowd.

Dancing music, loud noise, drinking chatter, laughter, and the smell of booze combined to make the weekend atmosphere to which Oscar and Louise exposed their son. Jack soon acquired a taste for beer, often sipping from his father's glass. Their friends thought it was cute and that it would teach him to hold his liquor later in life.

From time to time his parents experienced a twinge of conscience about the effect of this life on their child, but it was a voice they could turn off with the rationale that the entertainment money was needed for their living and Jack's future education.

The extra income was helpful and soon made possible the purchase of a small home. It was a white frame house at 14206 Liberal Avenue in Detroit, across the street from the Liberal Avenue Baptist Church. There was a garage next to the house. The main floor contained a kitchen, living room, and one bedroom. The Van Impes moved the kitchen to the basement and converted the former kitchen into a bedroom for Jack.

It was 1936. They had been in Detroit but two years and already owned their own home. They were pleased with their accomplishment in so short a time.

From his youth, Oscar had been associated with alcohol. It was a part of his life. Both in Belgium and in his new homeland he had felt free to indulge or refrain as he pleased. He had been intoxicated a number of times but never felt that booze had any hold on him. He hardly gave a second thought to the influence of being surrounded with drinkers every weekend and was surprised when it began to have an effect on him.

Pleasing the customers had its drawbacks. They were anxious to show their appreciation to their favorite entertainer and every treat meant another drink. The added intake of alcohol began to take its toll. At the end of an evening's performance Oscar was often well under the influence, but his rugged character and drive carried him through and the tavern owners didn't complain.

The night and day schedule was also difficult to live with. After playing the accordion and partying with friends until the early hours of the morning, Oscar had to summon all his strength just to roll out for work on Monday. An extra drink or two often helped him start the day.

Intrigued by the possibility of tremendous income and success in the entertainment field, Oscar began to plan a music education for his son. He could see Jack playing the accordion before great crowds. It thrilled him to think about it.

Oscar Van Impe is no visionary. Today, as a Christian, he is a rigid disciplinarian. Bible study is always a part of his day, and he spends at least two hours daily praying through a long prayer list, a task that has been started and discontinued by many a well-meaning Christian.

While he would be the first to give credit to His Lord as the One who enables him, there has always been a dogged determination about him and a will to succeed. He knew those dreams about his son's success as a musician were not enough. He understood the need of an early initiation to music, and long years of practice and study. So he decided to do his part by beginning to teach Jack the accordion at five years of age.

Today, when Dr. Van Impe does the triple bellows shake on the accordion he draws laughs from huge crowds by explaining that it was easy to learn to shake while his father stood over him with a club while teaching him to play. There is probably more truth than might be suspected in this tongue-in-cheek statement. Convinced that Jack had music in him, Oscar was determined to bring it out.

Remembering his own experience as a boy in Belgium he says that he had music in him but nobody would let it out. Through his early years he had begged for an instrument and was always tuned out by his parents. They shrugged off his pleas for music instruction laughingly. Discouraged, but with that characteristic determination, he kept after his father and finally was given an accordion when he was seventeen. It was as if he and the instrument were meant for each other. Once this was evident, he received encouragement from his family, a fact demonstrated by his father's investment in his expensive accordion purchased in America.

Perhaps that early hunger to play the accordion provided part of the incentive to help his son succeed musically. Whatever the drive, Oscar put his heart into those sessions with Jack and imparted to his five-year-old son a desire for perfection in performance that has never left him.

Oscar had no idea he was giving accordion lessons to a little boy who would later use his musical ability in Christ's service. Had he known those intense teaching times, when he was so weary from his factory and entertainment work, would produce a musician who would use his talent as a tool for evangelism he would have undoubtedly ceased Jack's instruction immediately.

Especially distasteful to Oscar were radio preachers and gospel musicians who, in his mind, cluttered up the air waves when he was trying to find his favorite program. How ironic that as he poured himself into the task of launching his son in a career of music with the aim of making him the world's greatest accordion player, he was actually equipping him musically for a world-wide radio and television ministry!

Night clubs, concerts, and the top stages of the world were all included in Oscar's goals as he pounded out rhythm with his student in that little house on Liberal Avenue. He had no way of knowing God would deliver his son from the best the world could offer so he could give God's great offer to the world in music and message.

Jack and the Chrysler – 6-7 yrs.

Jack – the prize-winning newsboy – 12 yrs.

CHAPTER FIVE

School Days

When five-year-old Jack Van Impe marched from his home on Liberal Avenue to nearby Gabriel Richard Grade School, it was like walking into a whole new world—a world of children. Being an only child, he had spent most of his life surrounded by adults. During the week he was in the constant company of his parents or an occasional sitter and on weekends he became part of the nightclub crowd, a grown-up group whose beer-hall behavior must have often been bewildering to a boy of five.

School days brought a communication problem for Jack. At home, his parents generally spoke Flemish, the Belgian tongue, while using English in public. Their son developed his own brand of Belgian English that served him well at home and in the company of his parents' friends but fell far short of the teacher's standards at Gabriel Richard. When he is extremely tired, Dr. Van Impe still reverts to that early way of speaking.

Young Jack wasn't impressed with the public school system. He was, in fact, so unimpressed that he was absent whenever possible. His entire grade school career is dotted with occasions when he chose to do things other than go to school.

One day, leaving his mother with his usual smile of innocence, he toddled off to kindergarten like an ideal student bent on an early start in education. Upon arriving at the playground, however, he chose a pleasant place among the shrubs that surrounded the school and waited out the morning. When the other children were dismissed, he simply joined the trek homeward, arriving right on time.

It was a clever maneuver for one so new at skipping school, but the young truant hadn't figured on the need of a note from his mother to get back into class the following day. That discovery moved him to more ingenious methods in the future.

At the beginning of World War II he even found a way to profit from patriotism in his campaign to escape the classroom.

The entire school had been recruited for a paper drive to help in the war effort. Jack was delighted at the opportunity to come to the aid of his country by being part of the group that gathered papers and magazines door to door on school time. He had great fun loading the trucks and jaunting around the neighborhood.

When the paper drive ended, and the school was back to business as usual, Jack's desk sat empty. Two weeks later, when he finally appeared for class, he was armed with a note from the school janitor (his friend) stating that he had been busy bundling papers all that time. Actually, the deceptive patriot had been relaxing on stacks of paper in the school basement reading hundreds of comic books that had been gathered in the paper drive.

Van Impe seems not to have been greatly influenced by others his age. He was a leader, not a follower. An instigator. A mover. Mischievous. Sometimes a real troublemaker.

Having easy access to whiskey in his home, Jack, like his father, ventured into bootlegging. In this grade school operation money was not the object nor was a "still" necessary for the manufacture of the devil's brew. The young booze peddler simply poured his potent product from his father's supply, packed it in Fletcher's Castoria bottles and gave it to his friends at school just to see how they would react. One classmate, after draining his laxative bottle filled with liquor, stood to recite and, to the teacher's dismay, fell sound asleep.

The Liberal Avenue Baptist Church, located across the street from the Van Impe home, was a special object of Jack's mischief. He disliked the loud singing sounding forth from the church on Sunday morning when his father was trying to sleep off Saturday night's drinking and entertaining. More than once the congregation found their service interrupted by overripe tomatoes and other missiles that came flying through open windows as Jack registered his opposition to their fervent worship.

Neighborhood stores were also victims of Jack and his friends. Shoplifting candy and other items became a way of life. They saw nothing wrong with helping themselves as long as they could get away with it.

To conclude from these incidents that Dr. Van Impe was just another tough street kid who spent all his time carousing Detroit's East Side looking for trouble would be a serious mistake. While it is true he was always looking for fun and excitement (sometimes less than wholesome) he was also a very busy, hard-working young man with more responsibilities than most his age; his father saw to that. While Oscar did not, at that time, know the verse existed, he practiced the philosophy of Lamentations 3:27: "It is good for a man that he bear the yoke in his youth."

Oscar had his son reading music at age four, and at five taking lessons with an hour each day set aside for practice. It was then he was given his first accordion.

Daily chores were always required. Jack carried out ashes, shoveled snow, mowed the lawn, and helped with his share of cooking and housework as soon as he was old enough to handle it.

He was also expected to do part of the week-end entertainment work. Furnished with a list of jokes, he became quite adept at drawing laughter from his nightclub audiences. Oscar, with his fine sense of timing, always saw that the hat was passed when the crowd was at its peak and captured by the young comedian. It was just good business.

Jack was taught early that drunks and their money should be parted, and a number of schemes were devised to make it happen. One was the old punchboard game where a charge was made for each punch, with the winner of the jackpot announced the following week. A fictitious name was always reported as the winner when the crowd gathered for the next drinking fest and the money went to the Van Impes. Oscar insisted it was perfectly all right to get ahead any way possible.

Had it not been for the grace of God, the night club work might have destroyed the future of this young entertainer. Though endowed with natural talent and loaded with energy, he was, even then, beginning to develop a taste for liquor. His family and friends were not disturbed by his drinking and even shared their booze with him, since he was too young to buy his own. Dr. Van Impe now recalls two occasions from those years when he was so intoxicated that he became unconscious and had to be carried to the family car after the performance.

Looking back, it is easy to pick out three major forces that shaped Jack Van Impe's life in those early years.

Oscar's discipline, drive, and desire to excel, have left an indelible mark. By both advice and example, this industrious father succeeded in teaching his son the importance of giving himself completely to any task worth beginning. He instilled in him a love for hard work that is without doubt a vital ingredient in his expanding ministry.

The quiet and tender nature of Louise also shows through. As a result of the steady increase in Oscar's drinking, and his heavy schedule, Jack was drawn more and more to his mother. Although Louise entered enthusiastically into the night club action, many times dancing all night, she drank less than most of the crowd and kept a clear head. Her son admired her and made a special effort to please her.

Though not enthused about his own studying, he assisted his mother in her preparation for U.S. citizenship and was thrilled with her success in naturalization.

Here is the source of Dr. Van Impe's ability to be compassionate and soft-spoken in appropriate moments in his ministering. The boisterous joy and boundless energy of his father combined with his mother's quiet nature have produced a personality ideally suited to the demands and needs of the work to which God has called him.

The night club crowd with its profanity, rowdiness, and cry

for a good time especially flavored his youth and resulted in the rough language and boredom with formal education that characterized those pre-conversion years. It is likely that his quick wit and sense of communication with large crowds were cultivated in those early appearances on night club stages. The fact that these abilities are now valuable in his ministry is another proof that God is able to make even the wrath of man praise Him (Psalm 76:10).

Another influence that deserves mention is that exerted by an accordion teacher named Peter Davey. He courageously accepted the task of preparing a nine-year-old dynamo to be a concert accordionist. Like Oscar, Mr. Davey was very strict. A perfectionist, he demanded excellence from his pupil. During his teaching time he kept a long pencil handy with which he cracked Jack's knuckles at each mistake. It was a powerful incentive for practice enough to appear with a flawless lesson. Though some might frown on Mr. Davey's method, he successfully produced a superb accordionist in seven years. He must be pleased with his accomplishment. The product of his instruction is heard by millions.

Like most American boys, Jack was intrigued by automobiles and other motorized means of getting around his world.

His first effort to graduate from less exciting modes of transportation (tricycles, bicycles, etc.) was at age seven when he discovered that his father's Model-A Ford would move, even without the key, by simply pressing the starter switch while the car was in gear.

One day his surprised parents returned, after leaving Jack with a sitter, to find him and the car in a field near their home. The young driver and his tired jalopy had arrived there a jump at a time and the battery was nearly depleted.

A few years later he induced his mother to be his accomplice in his drive to capture the family car. Assuring Louise that he had been watching his father carefully and had mastered the procedure, shifting and all, he invited her for a ride. He buttered her up with promises to take her places whenever she desired. It sounded good since Oscar's work schedule kept her confined during the week, so mother and son positioned themselves comfortably in Oscar's Chrysler sedan and Jack started the engine in preparation for the joyride.

There is no doubt that Oscar's son had indeed studied his father's shifting technique, a fact demonstrated by his ability to successfully get the car in reverse. He may well have taken in all the necessary know-how for highway driving and might have been able to chauffeur his mother around the neighborhood without difficulty. We will never know for sure, however, for somehow he had missed the knack of getting safely out of the garage.

Revving up the engine and popping the clutch, Jack roared halfway out of the garage before he crunched the Chrysler fender and ended the excursion.

Together, the two partners in this abortive driving attempt pushed the car back into the garage and Jack tried his hand at auto body work. He pounded the underside of the fender until it looked acceptable to his untrained eye and then painted it, thinking his father would never notice. Needless to say, the cover-up failed and both mother and son were the objects of Oscar's wrath that night.

In his early teens Jack traveled about the home area on a bright red Cushman motor scooter. It had a top speed of fifty miles an hour, but its owner kept trying to squeeze out fifty-five. Thankfully, he passed through the scooter stage uninjured.

Later, he tried motorcycling. A friend of the family left his Harley-Davidson with the Van Impes for a few months and gave Jack permission to use it. Those were exciting days, but they ended permanently when the friend returned for his bike.

Many of Dr. Van Impe's boyhood experiences were just that: everyday things that happen to millions of others which may not seem exciting or unusual and yet are the stuff of which life is made.

Had you visited him in those years you might have found him working on a model airplane in his room, playing ball in a vacant lot or on a school playground, wrestling with one of his friends, or headed for an afternoon at the movies.

Though he does not now attend the theater, he was a regular customer of the movie houses on Detroit's East Side when he was a boy. Nearly every Saturday and Sunday afternoon found him captured by the heroes of the silver screen.

He had worked out a circuit that would let him catch three shows in one afternoon. Louise often packed his lunch so he could follow the plan without interruption. His usual route took him to the "Ramona," the "Flamingo," and the "Eastwood" theaters.

In recent years thousands have stopped feeding on the modern offerings of Hollywood as a result of Dr. Van Impe's strong preaching on the subject.

Jack became a Boy Scout at the age of twelve and loved it. The uniform, the outings, and the projects with opportunities for recognition, were right down his alley and he ate it up. He gave himself to Scouting with typical enthusiasm and progressed to just two merit badges short of Eagle Scout, the highest award in scouting.

Caddying at the Lockmore Country Club became one of young Van Impe's first occupations. Although he has yet to play his first game of golf, he spent many hours toting golf bags for others. He worked hard, sometimes serving as many as four golfers at a time. The shortage of caddies in those war years offered good opportunity for boys who applied themselves, and ambition was one thing Jack has never lacked. He became a favorite at Lockmore and was often requested by the club members.

Another satisfying experience in Dr. Van Impe's youth was his job as a paper boy for the *Detroit News*. As a young businessman (age eleven), he threw himself into the task as if his success in life depended on it.

The average route for a newsboy at that time was thirty-five customers. As usual, Jack was not content to be average. His urge to excel sent him out seeking new business and within a few years he had built his paper route to 175 homes and had won the *Detroit News* newsboy contest for gaining new customers. The contest involved all the newsboys in the entire metropolitan area.

There were two driving forces that came into play in any Jack Van Impe project during his youth. One was that constant desire to excel and the other was an awful fear of failure. Jack just did not want to fail. Ever!

This haunting fear, while pushing him on to success in some cases, also kept him from a number of worthwhile undertakings. For example, he would never enter a contest for accordionists because he feared he might not place first among the contestants. Even though he was assured by his accordion teacher that he would win, Jack would not lay his talent on the line for fear of losing.

Now his fear has been replaced with faith, a courage builder that has enabled him to take on projects of immense scope and enormous responsibility.

Their European background, as well as their experience in the American depression, had made the Van Impes very money-conscious. Oscar was extremely frugal and, although he had built a good-sized bank account, he was determined that Jack should pay his own way as soon as possible. He knew this would teach his son responsibility in handling money and that the experience would help in later life. Therefore, Jack was responsible for purchasing all his own clothing after he reached his twelfth birthday.

It was also that year that Oscar and Louise wanted to buy new furniture for their son's room and offered to do so providing he would save enough to pay for half the cost of the new furnishings. Jack accepted the challenge and his room received a new look.

Following his parents' example and training, Jack was careful not to squander the money earned at his various part-time jobs. So well did he manage his money that at sixteen he paid $1,000 cash for an accordion. The accordion salesman could hardly believe his eyes when the teenage musician pulled the total amount out of an old boxing glove and handed it to him in payment for the instrument. When he was seventeen, Jack purchased a new Ford automobile with more savings. It is clear now that God was preparing a man He could trust with millions of dollars dedicated to carrying the gospel around the world.

There was very little emphasis on religion in the Van Impe home. Though there was a Catholic background from their family experience in Belgium, they seldom attended mass. Louise had taught Jack the child's prayer, "Now I lay me down to sleep," when he was very young and he had continued to pray that prayer daily for a number of years.

Later, he began to attend mass quite regularly with a neighbor family. Jack took his rosary and at that time began to think more about death. He began to add to his prayer: "Please, Lord, don't ever let my father, my mother, or me die." That continued until he started to feel that he was asking for the impossible. He saw that everyone would someday have to die. It was not until after he became a Christian that he understood how God could give eternal life to him and his loved ones.

As Jack approached the end of his grade school years he had an experience that so moved both he and his family that it must now be seen as an important step leading to their salvation.

It was a holiday weekend and Jack was not at the night club with his parents. He had been given a night out, with the understanding he would be home and in bed by 9 p.m. Louise had experienced an odd feeling about allowing him to go, but had dismissed it as nothing.

Ignoring his parents' instruction, Jack stayed out beyond their curfew and was crossing Gratiot Avenue, near his home, about 11 p.m. when he was struck by a speeding, reckless driver. He was thrown about thirty-five feet and landed face down on the pavement.

The incident nearly had a more tragic ending. The half-drunken occupants of the speeding car stopped and were stuffing the bleeding victim into the trunk of their car when they were arrested by a detective who had seen the accident.

Jack was taken to the Saratoga General Hospital and treated

for his injuries. Fortunately there were no lasting problems from the accident, but the Van Impe family attitude toward life and death was never quite the same after that. Dr. Van Impe feels God allowed the whole incident to prepare their hearts for receiving the gospel message.

As might be expected, God sent a man to minister to their ready hearts.

CHAPTER SIX

Born Again

Bill Rose had been fishing for men in the Plymouth Motor plant for a number of years. He had no idea that he would land a whopper like Oscar Van Impe whose influence for Christ, through his son, would reach around the world.

Oscar had been at the automobile factory for nine years before Bill's consistent witness began to affect him. It was 1943 and the world was uneasy. World War II was raging and the climate was one that incubated questions. When a man worked day after day producing machinery for the battlefield it forced him to think. Detroit, Michigan, the heart of America's war effort, was perhaps the most thinking city in the land. Bill moved among the workers in the "Fortress City" armed with hundreds of tracts on Bible prophecy and distributed his message with the zeal and passion of a soldier. Oscar read many of them with interest.

A number of experiences in Oscar's life had prepared him to receive the Gospel message. When he left Europe to come to America he thought he was on his way to the promised land, but arrived in a nation shaken to its roots by depression. He found himself struggling to survive. He had gone with Louise into the valley of the shadow of death as she brought his two children into the world and then had stood at the grave of his only daughter.

His dreams of success as an entertainer had moved him to begin his beer garden and night club work and had enabled him

Bill Rose
He witnessed to Oscar

Art Olsen
He led Jack
to Christ

Dr. John Hunter,
the Van Impe's pastor
at Liberal Avenue
Baptist Church

to lay aside a sizeable nest egg of cash, but he was growing tired of the drunkenness and noise of the crowds. Now, only a short time ago, his only son had narrowly escaped death. He was beginning to wonder what life was all about.

Interestingly, a factor in Oscar's conversion was a feature on the comic page of the paper that proposed looking 500 years into the future. Thinking about that, he wondered what he would be doing in 500 years.

At that time, he had no anticipation of heaven and found himself bothered by the thought that he might be in hell. He pushed the nightmare aside, but it returned. It wouldn't go away. He finally reasoned his way out of this awful fear by stating aloud: "I'll not be the only one there and if they can take it I can too."

It was slim comfort, but satisfied him for the moment.

It was shortly after this imaginary look into the future that Oscar sat down for lunch with Bill Rose on a bench in the carpenter's shop at the factory. Remembering that Bill was the fanatic who was always distributing religious literature, Oscar asked his lunch partner how he knew God existed.

"I know because the Bible says so," Bill answered.

"The Bible?" Oscar questioned. "Isn't that a bad book?"

"No," said Bill, "that's a good Book. It's God's Book."

"Well," replied Oscar, "I was taught it was a bad book and that you get crazy if you read it."

Bill saw his opportunity and took it. He began to unfold the teachings of the Bible to Oscar, telling him about his Lord and the way of eternal life. Oscar now recalls that Bill discussed salvation, heaven, hell, judgment, and the return of the Lord.

Bill didn't think he had accomplished much in that first discussion with Oscar and told his wife he thought Oscar would be tough to win. However, the object of his effort spent the evening excitedly sharing the information he had received with Louise

The next noon found Oscar back at the bench questioning his Bible instructor further. He was especially interested in prophecy. Eating it up. Here were answers to questions that had been lurking beneath the surface for a long time. He felt close to something important but couldn't yet grasp it.

The carpenter shop meetings continued for nearly four months. Bill Rose kept preaching faithfully to his congregation of one and prayed fervently for Oscar's salvation. Louise kept getting Bill's sermons second-hand each evening, digested, and somewhat Oscarized. It was the first time any one in Detroit had explained the gospel to the Van Impes.

The contrast between the wholesome Christian association with Bill Rose and the profane atmosphere of the weekend drinking crowd began to get to the part-time entertainer. Playing his accordion and looking out over a smoke-filled room one night, he remembers feeling that he was playing music in a morgue and saw the men and women before him as but the bodies of the dead. In recalling the awful experience he says: "I believe it was the Holy Spirit's way of showing me our spiritual death."

Soon after that eye opener, Oscar decided to take a month off from entertaining. The seven-day-a-week grind had been keeping him physically exhausted and, besides, he was weary from the spiritual struggle raging within. He needed time to think. Louise took a job for a short time on the night shift at Briggs Manufacturing, nearby, to keep their savings growing.

It was one of those nights, at home alone, that Oscar concluded he had delayed following Bill Rose's advice long enough. His friend had been urging him to receive Jesus Christ as his personal Saviour. Bill called it "being born again."

Searching out the old Bible they had found in the house at Freeport the year Jack was born, he began to look for verses that would enable him to understand what Bill had been talking about. He labored through a number of Old Testament chapters and found little help. He was still so unfamiliar with the Book that he didn't know where to look to end his search.

Laying the Bible gently aside, Oscar dropped to his knees. Truths from Bill's daily witnessing flooded his mind, yet he didn't know how to apply them. He felt filled with facts but without the wisdom to put them together in a way that would bring peace to his troubled heart. If only he could sort out a faith formula that would clear up his confusion!

Finally, he stopped struggling and took the only route that made sense to him. "Lord," he said, "if this man in the plant is telling me the truth, and this is real, and if you are willing to accept me and give me everlasting life, I want the Lord Jesus Christ to come into my heart."

The transaction between his soul and the Saviour went deeper than his words and in a few moments solid faith had replaced the "ifs" in his desperate prayer. He now knew what Bill had been talking about. The load was gone. He felt clean. New. Born again!

Rising from his knees, Oscar picked up the old Bible again. That old book with torn and missing pages would become his food and drink in the weeks to come as he explored the mysteries of his new life.

When Louise returned from work Oscar told her about his experience. She listened politely but wondered if Oscar's religion would last.

The next day Oscar shared the good news of his salvation with Bill Rose. Bill was overjoyed. He had witnessed and prayed so long and had become utterly discouraged at times, yet Oscar had finally responded to his testimony. It had been worth it all. They rejoiced together and were thankful God had caused their paths to cross.

For the next several days Louise watched and wondered. Oscar had stopped drinking entirely. His temper was under control. He was so changed in his feeling about honesty that he returned a number of items he had brought home from the Plymouth plant. He read the Bible often, almost constantly in those first days of new life. She really didn't know what to make of it, but remembers feeling good about the change in his life. Still, she dismissed the thought that this same thing might happen to her.

Nevertheless, a few days later she found herself walking down a church aisle with Oscar as he publicly acknowledged his faith in Christ. Louise came forward with him responding to the invitation to be saved. They were now one in Christ as well as in marriage. Oscar was thrilled beyond words and Mr. and Mrs. Bill Rose looked on with evident satisfaction and joy. It was a little taste of heaven for them all.

The youngest of the Van Impes, while absent at the moment of decision for both Oscar and Louise, observed the results with interest. He saw that something good had happened to his parents and wanted to get in on it. The week following his mother's conversion Jack told his father he wanted to be saved.

Pleased with the work of God in his son's heart, yet feeling inadequate to lead him to Christ, Oscar told Jack to go to the little Baptist church across the street from their home and ask how to be born again.

It must have been an interesting view from heaven. Here was the boy who had despised the fervent singing of the Christians in the Liberal Avenue Baptist Church, now walking up the front steps of that very church an hour before Sunday School was to start, searching for someone who could lead him to Christ.

There were only a few people present when young Jack Van Impe walked in that morning. His steps echoed in the near-empty auditorium and the noise made him self-conscious. Slowly, he made his way down the aisle to the pulpit where the Sunday School superintendent was preparing for the coming session.

Mr. Ernest, the superintendent, looked up in pleasant surprise when his young visitor spoke. He was about to give the boy a warm Sunday School welcome but was interrupted by the earnest youth announcing that he had come to be saved. It was the kind of interruption good Sunday School superintendents pray for, but seldom expect.

He listened with joy as Jack told him about the miracles that had changed his family and heard him explain how his father had sent him to find someone more experienced in spiritual things who could tell him how to be saved.

Mr. Ernest knew just the man. Art Olsen, a soldier home on

furlough, had also arrived early and was praying in a small prayer room off the church auditorium. He led Jack there without further delay and explained the situation to the dedicated Christian soldier.

There couldn't have been a better man for Jack to meet in his time of spiritual urgency than Art Olsen. Art loved his Lord and he loved souls. There is no question but that this encounter had been timed by God.

Art opened his Bible, worn from much use, and went carefully through the plan of salvation. Jack was a sinner. God loved him in spite of his sin. Jesus came into the world to save sinners, shedding His blood on the cross. Dying for Jack. Risen from the grave, He invites sinners to turn from sin and receive Him as Saviour and Lord. Was that what Jack wanted to do?

When the answer came a clear and definite "Yes!" Art knew that no more explanation was needed. They knelt together on that hard, uncarpeted wood floor and Jack Van Impe placed his faith in the Lord Jesus Christ, inviting Him into his heart.

When they rose from their knees, Jack knew that he had found the reason for the change in his parents' lives, and although they were not present, he felt even closer to them than before. And with good reason—they now all belonged to the family of God.

He also knew that he had established a strong bond with the soldier who had knelt beside him. It was to be a great friendship based on the boy's continuing respect for the man who had become his spiritual father. In years to come, Art Olsen's name would be mentioned by a Bible-quoting evangelist whenever his personal testimony was given. Art would always be glad for having arrived early to pray on that important Lord's Day morning.

Jack remained at the church through the morning service. It was all very strange to him, having never been in a Protestant service before, but his heart was so full that he joined in the singing like a long-time saint. He remembers they sang: "RING THE BELLS OF HEAVEN" and "I AM HAPPY IN THE

SERVICE OF THE KING." How significant! A young new Christian stood among them who would give his entire life to the service of the King.

When the pastor gave the invitation at the close of the message, a very happy twelve-year-old boy stepped out into the aisle and walked to the front of the church to publicly acknowledge his faith in Jesus Christ. The people rejoiced and heaven was glad. Jack Van Impe was born again.

CHAPTER SEVEN

Family on Fire

A few weeks after their conversions, the Van Impes were baptized at the Liberal Avenue Baptist Church. They had decided to make it their church home. Its location, directly across the street from their home, and the warm Biblical ministry of Pastor John Hunter convinced them to settle there.

Few knew that the dark-eyed boy being immersed in the baptistry that night was the culprit who had thrown tomatoes through the church windows during services in earlier days. Many years later, his courage increased, Jack Van Impe returned to his home church to preach and asked if anyone remembered being hit by a tomato during a church service. Two hands shot up and the offender rendered a tardy confession.

The victims, long over the effects of the mischief, rejoiced in the work of God in the life of the young man who had grown up among them. Many congregations would be willing to endure the persecution of a little flying fruit from hecklers if the result would be the conversion of another Jack Van Impe.

It is ironic that Dr. Van Impe grew up on Liberal Avenue, was saved and baptized at the Liberal Avenue Baptist Church, and became an uncompromising fundamentalist evangelist known around the world for his solid Bible preaching and his opposition to theological liberalism.

Evidently Pastor Hunter also disliked the "liberal" label and under his leadership the church became the Ambassador Baptist Church. When Jack and Rexella Van Impe began their evangelistic work as a team they traveled under the name of "Ambassadors for Christ."

Though the word "liberal" has never fit the Van Impe position on Bible doctrine or interpretation, it does describe the new attitude that Oscar had toward money and material things after his conversion. Formerly an example of frugality and tight-fisted stinginess, he now became a giver. Within a few months after his new birth he had given away all his savings with the exception of some U.S. savings bonds.

Dr. DeHaan's Radio Bible Class and Dr. Charles E. Fuller's Old Fashioned Revival Hour were a few of the beneficiaries of Oscar's liberality. Dr. Van Impe says: "I have never known a man who gives like my father. If you give him ten dollars for his birthday it will probably end up on the mission field."

Rev. Hunter soon sensed that he had an unusual family in his congregation and encouraged them in their fervent witnessing. His solid ministry and counsel exerted a lasting influence on these babes who were determined to devour the entire Bible and win the world for Christ, singlehandedly if necessary.

Oscar was so thrilled with his salvation that he set out at once to share it with others, especially his fellow workmen and his Belgian friends from the night club life.

He had thousands of tracts printed containing the story of their conversion, and he mailed these throughout the Belgian community. Such a stir was caused when the tracts arrived in the mail on the same day that many Belgian families passed on the street hurrying to one another's homes to tell what had happened to Oscar and his family.

The word spread through the Plymouth plant like wildfire. The new convert had great courage and sometimes was surrounded by thirty-five to forty men all asking questions about his conversion or the Bible. He knew little of God's Word but enthusiastically gave his testimony and shared what truth he had absorbed from the months of listening to Bill Rose and from his limited study during the few weeks following his salvation experience.

Even those who passed by the Van Impe residence were

exposed to the gospel message. A sign made with twelve-inch letters and placed on the front of the house announced: "JESUS SAVES." All the neighbors knew that something revolutionary had happened at 14206 Liberal Avenue. And the Van Impes left no doubt as to the reason for the transformation. They had been saved, born again, converted, or whatever other Biblical term best described salvation to their listeners. They declared themselves on the Lord's side and they wanted everybody to know it.

The accordion had played a vital part in the life of this family for more than nine years. It had been both a source of enjoyment and a means of livelihood. Now it seemed to stand for the old life. Oscar and Jack packed their precious instruments away with a note of sadness, willing to do whatever pleased their Lord. Then one Sunday afternoon, an unforgettable experience enlisted their musical ability in the service of the King.

Oscar had decided to lie down for an afternoon nap. He had been so busy working and witnessing that he was exhausted and felt the need of rest. To relax, he tuned the radio to a station with quiet orchestra music and stretched out to listen and unwind.

After the events of the day and week had stopped tumbling through his tired mind, Oscar found his thoughts focusing on the half-filled auditorium of their little church. As he meditated on the rows of empty pews, he suddenly pictured the huge crowds that gather to hear the beautiful music of the famous orchestras such as was then being broadcast into his home.

Almost before he realized it, tears began running down his cheeks and soon he was sobbing heavily. "Why should all the beautiful music be wasted?" he cried. "Why couldn't the Lord use good music for his work?"

Oscar continued to weep for some time and Louise became alarmed. But there was nothing to fear. This moving experience she was witnessing was her husband's surrender of his musical talent and all his ability and energy to the service of his Lord.

A few days later, at a tent evangelistic meeting sponsored by the Gratiot Avenue Baptist Church, Oscar was given the opportunity to play the accordion and give his testimony. He was on his way. The world would hear more of him, both in his own evangelistic work and, in the following years, through the worldwide ministry of his son.

In a quieter but effective way, Louise also gave herself to the work of Christ. Always at Oscar's side, she supported him in his zeal to reach the Belgian community. By mailing thousands of tracts and letters she shared in the gospel outreach.

Her special quality of compassion moved her to send over seven thousand envelopes containing appropriate tracts to the families of servicemen whose names appeared in the war casualty lists published in the newspaper.

Jack, while still all boy, began to use his boundless energy in witnessing for Christ. The day he was saved he zeroed in on the fellows in his young gang. Meeting them in their favorite hideaway, he insisted that they all accept Christ as Saviour or face the consequences. Like the Emperor Constantine, who marched his armies into rivers to be baptized by regiments hoping to make them Christians, Jack thought he could do the Lord's work by hand. Better methods were adopted later.

Playing his accordion alongside his father in revival meetings, church services, youth rallies, and evangelistic crusades the young accordionist gained valuable experience for his future ministry and increased in Bible knowledge through hearing many able and gifted men of God.

True dedication often has brought Christians persecution. The Van Impes were no exception. Many friends would have nothing more to do with them. Stories that they had lost their minds circulated through the Belgian community. Oscar was the object of much ridicule in the factory.

Without doubt, the most difficult reaction to accept was that of Oscar's family in Belgium. The word that floated back to Europe from their former friends was that Oscar and his family in America had become religious fanatics. His father was furious. Letters that came from their loved ones attacking them for their stand for Christ brought much grief to their hearts, and often tears to their eyes. Knowing the reaction was the result of spiritual blindness, Oscar, Louise, and Jack, kept faithfully serving Christ and praying for the day they would see their family in Belgium saved.

The Plymouth plant, the night club crowd, and the friends and relatives of the Van Impes all felt the impact of their testimony. Since Dr. Van Impe was saved at the very outset of his teen years, the Edwin Denby High School was next in line for an encounter with the youngest member of the family on fire for God.

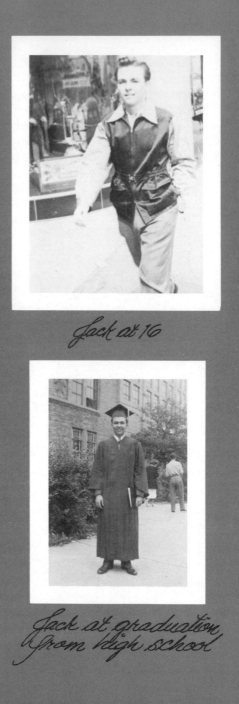

Jack at 16

Jack at graduation from high school

CHAPTER EIGHT

This One Thing I Do!

If the administrators at Edwin Denby High studied the records of students entering from Gabriel Richard Grade School, they must have had difficulty believing the background of ninth grader Jack Van Impe. The former reluctant learner and persistent truant arrived promptly each day and appeared to be doing well in all his classes.

While some may have concluded that sudden maturity had set in, the real reason for the change in this energetic, dark-eyed, young man was his conversion to Jesus Christ. That experience had reshaped his values and had given new purpose and direction to his life. Already, he knew he was headed for full-time service for Christ and he wanted to be adequately equipped. The desire to excel that had called forth his best in work and music now began to show in the classroom.

Immediately following his salvation, Jack had become active in the Liberal Avenue Baptist Church. Pastor John Hunter's helpful instruction and personal interest were of great importance in those first months, as was his family's zeal to serve the Lord. At home, he literally lived in an atmosphere of revival. These dynamic influences, combined with his association with other dedicated youth at the church, sent the young evangelist-to-be to high school determined to be a Christian example as a student and to capture the campus for Christ.

Lee Vandenberg was one fellow student who was exposed to Jack's fervent witnessing. He sat directly behind Jack in the study hall at Denby and was one day surprised when his neighbor in front turned and said: "Lee, you don't look too happy. You need the Lord!" Jack felt he had failed in his blunt witness and remembers thinking: "I tried, but that kid will probably never be saved." Lee is now the pastor of the First Baptist Church of Flushing, Michigan and was chairman of the large and successful crusade Dr. Van Impe held there recently.

Jack's closest friends in those years were David Baer and Marvin Poelke. Dave and Marv were in the youth group at the church and shared their friend's zeal to witness for Christ. The three were locker partners and kept their common cabinet stocked with gospel tracts, which they openly distributed in the halls and classrooms of the school.

Even class assignments became opportunities to tell the gospel to other students and teachers. A speech that would otherwise have been "just more school work" took on the flavor of a sermon. Themes and essays were generally done on Bible subjects or explained the miracle that had taken place in the Van Impe home, the writer feeling pleased that his teacher would be required to read his testimony when grading the paper.

Anxious to present a clear witness and to properly prepare himself for the Lord's work, Jack studied so diligently that he often nearly memorized the lesson text. His straight "A" high school average testifies to the quality of his work, and the study habits developed in those years have been of immense value in his ministry.

In contrast to his dubious deportment in grade school, Jack set high standards for himself in both dependability and punctuality. He was neither late nor absent during his entire high school career. He has held to these habits in his ministry and has never once missed a service, even when ill.

Though eager to share his faith at every opportunity, young Van Impe was not a born preacher who naturally took to the pulpit and captivated his hearers. A brief book-report-testimony in high school is a far cry from a polished sermon and the day came when he found that to be true.

Pastor Hunter, sensing he had a minister in the making,

arranged for his prodigy to preach to all the youth of the church. Seizing the opportunity, Jack prepared with diligence. Devouring books and making exhaustive notes, he finally felt fully prepared for the occasion. The speaking time in the meeting was to be twenty minutes, which seemed too short a time for such expected eloquence armed with so much inspired information.

Consulting his notes for the opener, the fifteen-year-old preacher launched his first sermon in confidence. Six minutes later he was surprised to find that he had finished his material. Undaunted, he shuffled his notes and started again, using up exactly the same amount of time. Now a bit rattled, he brought his talk to an end, with eight minutes to spare. Alas, his sermon had become a sermonette. Today, he fills every available minute and longs for more time to preach the unsearchable riches of Christ.

When, in his high school years, Jack Van Impe visualized himself in Christian work, it was always in a musical ministry. He anticipated a life of travelling with famous evangelists, providing music for their meetings. That ambition spurred him on in his music education and enabled him to discipline himself for hours of practicing.

In the first few years of high school he practiced two hours daily. Later he increased to four hours. It was then the real breakthrough came that has led to the excellence in performance known to crusade congregations around the world.

It's trite, but true, that experience is the best teacher. And Dr. Van Impe's teens were filled with opportunities for experience as a Christian musician. He was in constant demand for special music in youth rallies, church services, and revival meetings. When the demand was lacking, Oscar created it. Sometimes more than his son desired.

Oscar would scour the newspaper each night in search of advertisements of gospel services where he and Jack could play their accordions and give their testimonies. As their reputation for quality music grew, the openings came easily.

On one such occasion, Oscar scheduled a meeting at the last

minute and informed Jack they were to play their accordions for a service. Jack, just into his teens, had plans to play ball that evening and was weary from several nights of meetings, but he reluctantly accompanied his father to the service.

It was Oscar's habit to warm up the crowd a bit with lively songs and some comments about being happy in the Lord. As usual, he positioned Jack on one side of the pulpit and he on the other. Looking then across the pulpit he shouted, "Are you happy, my son?"

"No!" shouted honest Jack, in front of nearly five hundred people! The crowd exploded. Oscar did his best to rescue the situation, but it was difficult. That night, following the service, there was a father-son conference that Dr. Van Impe will never forget.

With such a busy schedule of meetings and an unusual conscientiousness about his school work, one might think there was no time for normal social life in Jack Van Impe's high school years. Not true; there were many good times in that period of his life.

Always involved in his church youth group, Jack was there whenever the teens gathered for activities. Their youth fellowship, though not large, was extremely busy and sometimes joined with other churches of like faith for outings and rallies. Most often they met with the youth from the Burns Avenue Baptist Church, the mother church of their own.

It was at just such a fellowship that Jack became acquainted with two young men who have continued to be his friends through the years. Stanley Koenke later traveled with him to Belgium as part of a Youth For Christ team. Rudy Schuermann, now director of Victorious Life Ministries at Pontiac, Michigan, accompanied and worked with him in a number of services in his Bible training years and still remains a valued friend and brother in the ministry. Dr. Van Impe speaks of Rudy as a trusted fellow-laborer who can be counted on in any time of need.

Jack dated a number of young ladies, often double dating

with Stanley or Rudy and their girl friends. His standards were exceptionally strict and he never would date a girl who was not a Christian. Pastor Hunter had emphasized the importance of not being unequally yoked with unbelievers (II Corinthians 6:14), and Jack had taken it to heart.

Feeling now a burden to stress this truth to youth everywhere, he often hammers on this point to audiences having a great number of young people.

Jack's "wheels" consisted of his father's 1933 Chrysler. The old car ran well and was very dependable. Strangely, it was one of the reasons for his strict rules on dating for both he and his friends.

Shortly after his conversion, Oscar had placed a large sign on the back of the car that announced: "JESUS SAVES." Like the one on his house, it carried the family testimony to all. That sign placed a great responsibility on the teenage son in the family, and he accepted it! He felt that all activity in that automobile must be consistent with the sign on the back. Therefore, he forbade any kissing in his car and would not even allow dates to sit too close to one another, lest some observer misread their intentions.

What a wise father Oscar was! Had the effect of his sign become known to parents in those days there might have been a run on gospel mottos that would have exhausted the supply of all Christian bookstores in the land.

Jack was also careful to maintain a testimony with dates outside the family car. He chuckles when he recalls one experience at a date's door. As he was about to leave, he said, "I'll be praying for you."

"Is that all?" she asked.

"No," he added, "I'll write you occasionally."

"Is that all?" she repeated.

"No" he answered, taking her hand and looking deeply into her eyes: "God bless you, sister."

And with that he turned politely and walked to the waiting automobile.

Strange standards, you say. Perhaps. Certainly to the majority, Yet, nothing succeeds like success. And who can deny that Dr. Van Impe has enjoyed a blessed and successful life?

Though changed completely in attitude at his conversion, the mischievous personality remains. Sanctified, but still there.

One night in passing Stanley Koenke's girlfriend's house he noticed his friend's car in the drive. Leaving the old Chrysler a block down the street he returned on foot and, finding the keys in the ignition, roared off with Stanley's car. When Stanley heard his car motor revving up he guessed it to be Jack and wasn't at all concerned.

After a joyride for a few blocks Jack returned the car to the drive and went back to his own waiting automobile, only to be confronted by a policeman who had witnessed the whole thing.

By this time, Stanley had left the house and, passing the Van Impe car, stopped to inquire why the police were there. Unfortunately neither boy had registrations with them for the cars and they were both hauled off to the police station where they were kept and questioned for a considerable time.

Finally, the police were able to contact Stanley's father, who vouched for the boys and brought about their releases. It was the closest Dr. Van Impe has ever come to spending the night in jail.

Like most sons who use their father's cars, Jack one day had a minor accident with the old Chrysler. Entering the drive with some hesitation after the accident, Jack remembered his father's reaction to his childhood driving experience. Thankful that Oscar was now a Christian who was constantly praising the Lord, Jack decided to put his father's joy to a test.

Entering the door, he shouted, "Praise the Lord, Dad!" Oscar sensed that something was wrong and questioned his son about his sudden burst of joy. Jack then led him outside to the damaged car with another "Praise the Lord, Dad! I had an accident with the car."

Oscar's response was characteristic of the new man he had become. Placing his arm around Jack's shoulder he replied: "Praise the Lord, son! We're not going to let the devil have the victory!" And they didn't! Jack would never forget his father's Christian reaction and has shared it with thousands when giving his conversion story in crusades.

Meanwhile, back at the Plymouth plant, Oscar had been evangelizing with the same zeal that his son was displaying at Edwin Denby High. He had given out tracts by the thousands and was well known throughout the factory for his consistent Christian testimony and his constant joy.

Some mocked. "Praise the Lord!" they would shout when Oscar entered their work area.

"Amen, but I wish you meant it like I do!" was Oscar's usual reply.

But the Lord was not going to allow this blessed Belgian to make automobiles all his life. He had too much to give, and an obedient heart ready to go. God called Oscar out of the Plymouth plant and sent him to Detroit Bible Institute (now Detroit Bible College) in the year that his son was a sophomore in high school. Both father and son went to school each morning with a single goal in mind—that of being prepared to serve their Lord wherever He should send them.

Oscar's enrollment at Detroit Bible College changed the financial picture drastically for the Van Impes. They had given away all their savings except for $2,500 in U.S. Savings Bonds. These they now began to cash when absolutely necessary. Oscar was sure the Lord had called him to prepare for the ministry so he felt confident their needs would somehow be supplied.

Jack was anxious to help his parents in their preparation for the Lord's service and held a number of part-time jobs to add to the family income. As might be expected, opportunities came that were beyond his asking. Work opened that not only aided in the family budget but allowed him to save money for a new accordion and, in the summer following his senior year, to purchase a new car.

In the first part of his high school career, Jack continued his work on the paper route. Later, he added other jobs. An average summer day might have found him setting out fruit at 8:00

a.m. at the corner grocery, caddying at the Lockmore Country Club or selling plastic clothespins door to door, and returning to the store to take in the fruit display at 9:00 p.m.

On Saturday he gave accordion lessons, travelling to his students on his red Cushman motor scooter. Earnings from his many jobs earned him an average of $125 weekly during the summer season, a wage above that earned by many breadwinners at that time.

Jack Van Impe graduated from Edwin Denby High School in the spring of 1948. He had enjoyed a full and fruitful high school career. When he crossed the platform to receive his diploma, he felt pleased with his accomplishment and enthusiastic about the future.

Already an invitation to travel for the entire summer had come and he had accepted. He would be the summer musician for evangelist Leonard Thompson, ministering in Michigan, Ohio, and Illinois.

In the fall he would attend Detroit Bible College where Oscar had, this very year, graduated with honors. Confident that God had planned a wonderful future for him, he was eager to get on with it.

CHAPTER NINE

Study To Show Thyself Approved

Like kindergarten, Bible school was a whole new world. A world inhabited by Christians.

Jack Van Impe had now come full circle. He had moved from the unsaved, drinking crowd in Detroit's night clubs to the Christian fellowship of Detroit Bible College. It was like a taste of heaven.

Finally, he had arrived at his chosen place of training for the Lord's work. Although his aim was still primarily a musical ministry, he wanted to take in all the Bible he could in order to assist in meetings whenever possible. He determined to apply himself as he had in high school so as to be well-equipped for the service of the King.

Some of the courses in this new place of learning were real mind bogglers. Theology, Hermeneutics, Exegesis, Greek, and other frightening names appeared on the list of classes available. Jack, of course, had the advantage of drawing on his father's experience and knew something about the meaning of such high-sounding subjects. He was confident he would be able to handle them.

After the secularism of high school, it was refreshing to find each class beginning with prayer and to feel the instructors really cared. Chapel was especially helpful, with outstanding speakers and musicians often ministering to the students.

He felt at home.

Many new and lasting friendships were formed in those years

67

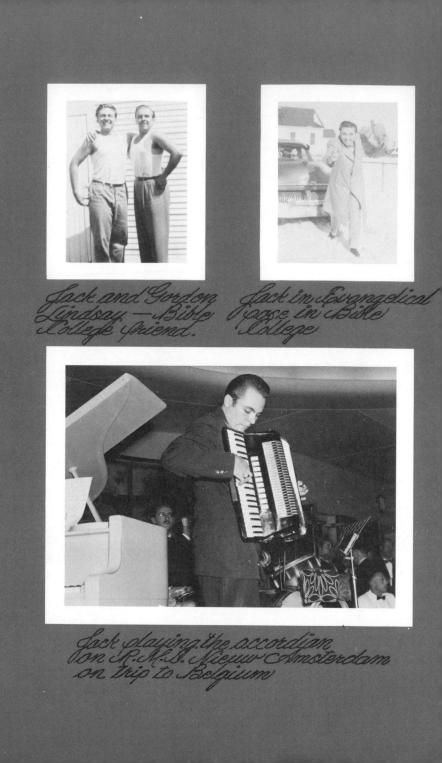

Jack and Gordon
Lindsay — Bible
College friend.

Jack in Evangelical
pose in Bible
College

Jack playing the accordion
on R.M.S. Nieuw Amsterdam
on trip to Belgium

at D.B.C. Pastors, missionaries, and teachers in different parts of the world look back with joy, as does Dr. Van Impe, to those days of that small student body bound together in Christian fellowship. There is no question but that this was God's place for the training of his servant.

That Jack Van Impe had come to study was evident from the excellence of his work in every class. II Timothy 2:15 seemed to fit his purpose as a student from the beginning: "Study to show thyself approved unto God, a workman that needeth not to be ashamed, rightly dividing the word of truth" (II Timothy 2:15).

There was one frustrating fact about being in a total Christian atmosphere: there was no one to whom he could witness. Throughout his high school career he had been pursuing souls. Evangelizing! Now everyone around him was already converted. He began to feel like a salesman without prospects. Realizing there were thousands outside the school walls in need of Christ, he began to join with others in witnessing teams. One of his friends, Gordon Lindsay, became a close co-laborer in reaching out to the lost.

Since Gordon was preparing to preach and Jack to minister in music, they made a good combination. Gordon grabbed every speaking opportunity and Jack provided the music, leading the singing and playing the accordion. So successful was this arrangement that the next summer vacation they traveled together as an evangelistic team.

Holding one-night and week-long crusades, these two dedicated young men served with all their hearts. What they didn't yet have in experience they made up in zeal and God blessed their efforts with souls and gave them priceless training for their later ministries.

Besides their love for the work of Christ, Jack and Gordon had another common problem: they were both fighting the battle of the bulge. It was extremely easy for them to add pounds. Sometimes conscientious about the situation, and more often ignoring it, they went from feast to famine. Dr. Van Impe recalls that one week might find them buying donuts and rolls by the dozen and the next they would be on a grapefruit diet.

Nevertheless, both men have good memories about their labor together in the Lord's harvest.

Jack and Gordon were sometimes partners in mischief as well as in ministry. One object of their antics was a good student named Charles Wagner, who was especially anxious to do well in the class taught by Dr. David Allen, who was also the young man's pastor.

Knowing this, the two buddies somehow got their hands on an examination paper being returned to their fellow student by Dr. Allen. They carefully changed the "A" on the paper to an "F" and then went through the paper with a teacher's marking pencil and made supposed comments by Dr. Allen about the poor fellow's answers.

Since Dr. Allen taught only every other day, and the paper arrived on the off day, the embarrassed classmate stewed for a whole day before his tormentors confessed and laughed with him. He laughed weakly. The episode evidently didn't harm the victim. Dr. Charles Wagner has had an especially successful ministry and is now president of Northwest Baptist Seminary in Tacoma, Washington.

On other occasions, these good friends enjoyed playing pranks on each other. A magician named "Waldo" was making the Detroit circuit at that time, and Gordon arrived at the school bulletin board one day to find an ordination certificate posted with the following message: THIS IS TO CERTIFY THAT GORDON LINDSAY WAS ORDAINED TO THE MINISTRY BY WALDO THE MAGICIAN.

On a better day, Gordon Lindsay was ordained to the ministry and has served for more than twenty-five years as pastor of one fine church, the Five Points Community Church near Pontiac, Michigan.

Though a serious student, the Van Impe sense of humor had to surface from time to time. Occasionally it was in the classroom.

Dr. Roy Aldrich, who wrote a few years ago congratulating his former student on receiving his doctorate, once made Jack stand in the corner for an entire class period. He had been cutting up in theology class and the good professor concluded the juvenile punishment might shape up the young attention-getter.

Dr. Shaw, professor of Bible archeology, once called Jack aside and told him he was an excellent student but should learn to take better notes in class. The next day Jack arrived with a portable typewriter and started pounding away while Prof. Shaw lectured. When asked what he was doing, Jack answered, "Taking better notes."

The understanding attitude of these godly instructors must not be overlooked. Seeing the potential of their sometimes mischievous student, they worked with him. His consistency in handling their most difficult assignments demonstrated an earnest desire to learn, despite his periodic cutting up.

Their recognition of this fact is commendable and shows genuine Christian maturity within the teaching staff. It is clear they were at Detroit Bible College to serve the Lord, not just to fill a position in Christian work. Only eternity will reveal the powerful influence these faithful servants exerted on Jack Van Impe and others who now minister God's Word in different areas of the world.

One Bible instructor particularly effective in shaping Dr. Van Impe's life was Dr. David Allen. This pastor of the dynamic and growing Calvary Baptist Church of Hazel Park, Michigan, brought both knowledge and experience to the classroom. His impact on the students was considerable.

Jack was deeply impressed with Dr. Allen's ability to quote the Scriptures from memory. Sitting in his class was an experience in absorbing the Bible. It was inevitable; theory and opinion were always on the back burner. The Bible itself was given priority.

Word studies took the students on Biblical treasure hunts, with Dr. Allen tying the Old and New Testaments together in unforgettable fashion. Tracing doctrinal foundations were not long and dull readings from church history, but a constant comparison of Scripture texts that allowed the students to build on a solid foundation. Walking out of the classroom, the young

71

ministers and missionaries-to-be often visualized themselves giving out the sacred text in the interesting manner mastered by their able instructor.

Jack sometimes attended Dr. Allen's church and from time to time was used as a musician in the services. Later, he felt honored to be featured on various Bible conference programs with his former Bible College teacher. They have remained good friends through the years and Dr. Allen recently wrote the following, commending the ministry of his former student:

I have known Dr. Jack Van Impe for over twenty-five years and have followed his ministry from its beginning.

It has been thrilling to see how the Lord has used his talents in an ever increasing way. It is obvious that the Lord's hand is upon the unusual ministry of Jack Van Impe.

He is being used to reach the masses by his crusades, the radio, and television.

We fundamentalists are glad to be able to back an evangelist who does not compromise with the ecumenical movement nor the charismatics.

Signed—David D. Allen

During his Bible College years, Jack lived at home and commuted to school. The two primary reasons for his choice of the college were the enthusiasm of his father over the teaching program there and the financial savings in living at home. The bond between this close-knit family remained strong and Jack was vitally involved in the missionary ministry that was being developed by his parents at that time.

Oscar and Louise had come to America to get rich and had gained something far more important than wealth when they were born again. Their lives were so changed that they wanted to share the good news with the world.

The special part of the world that lay heavy upon their hearts was the place of their birth, the country of Belgium. Relatives there were all unsaved and they longed to go to them with the message of Christ.

Immediately after graduation from the Bible College, they began to plan their missionary journey. Visiting churches and individuals, they tried to build a constituency of praying and supporting people who would share the burden of their hearts.

Slowly, interest began to develop in a number of friends and churches for one of the most neglected mission fields in the world. Belgium, a country of 10 million people, has but a tiny touch of biblical Christianity. In the town where Oscar's family lived there was not one born-again person, to the best of their knowledge. The Van Impes purposed to do something about that, and laid their strategy for crossing the sea again, this time in search of souls.

Their son did his part by gaining prayer support among his friends at the college and in presenting the need whenever possible. He also continued to share some services with his father, contributing to the cause through his accomplished work on the accordion.

Funds come slowly for missionary work in areas that are not generally thought of as mission fields. Even while in Belgium as missionaries, their monthly income never exceeded $250. Still, month after month, the number of praying partners increased and the money trickled in. Encouraged, Oscar bought a station wagon for travel in his former homeland and set a tentative departure date.

As the time of his parents' venture approached, Jack had mixed feelings. He was completely convinced of the need and felt his father's knowledge of the language and the people would enable him to have an effective ministry. He knew that Oscar and Louise had prayed much about the will of God in the matter, as had he, yet he found himself dreading the day of their departure.

The Korean War was being fought at that time and Jack felt there was a strong possibility it might finally engulf other parts of the world. Political unrest was evident in Belgium and he wondered how this would affect his loved ones. They were the only relatives he had known up to this time in his life and the thought of their departure was not easy for him to bear. Still, preparations continued.

Oscar knew that he was acting in the Lord's will and was so confident in his son's competency that he arranged to leave everything in Jack's charge. The house was his to do with as he thought best. There were no funds to leave, but Oscar was sure that Jack would have enough money available through his accordion work to pay the bills and continue his education. It was clear that he had peace in his heart about his actions and that he trusted his Lord would not fail him.

It would be difficult to describe Jack Van Impe's feelings on that August day in 1950 as his parents loaded the new station wagon to leave for Belgium. The plan was to drive to New York and ship the car and baggage so they would be well equipped on their arrival. The moment had finally arrived. The missionary journey to Europe was beginning.

Oscar opened the car door and turned to embrace his only son. Jack stood there weeping. All the family he had ever known was about to leave him. He felt alone. Not sure about their safety. Empty.

Oscar held him close and said: "Listen, Jack, the Lord is coming soon, and if we don't see you anymore here, we'll meet up there." Jack nodded, without answering. His father turned back to the waiting car and waved another farewell. Louise, like her son, wiped away the tears as they headed down Liberal Avenue. Jack stood silently and watched them until they were out of sight.

Taking a deep breath and straightening his shoulders, the only Van Impe left in Detroit walked slowly toward the empty house. There was no time to spend worrying or grieving. He must assume all the responsibilities of both a homeowner and student. There were bills to pay, errands to run, books to study, and plans to make. He had a duty to his parents and a commitment to Christ. Both must be fulfilled. It was time to be about his business.

Soon after his family left for Belgium, Jack rented the house to a dependable couple, reserving a room for himself. It was a wise move, providing both income and a lessening of responsibility. Oscar's faith had been justified. He had raised a son with a good head for business, an asset that has also been of great value in the responsibilities given him by his heavenly Father.

With the income from the rental, and honorariums given him for his many musical appearances, he managed well. Word from his parents telling of their safe arrival and the beginning of their missionary work set his mind at ease. When the news came of the conversion of his grandparents, his heart was full. He knew the Van Impes were on target. In God's will.

He didn't feel alone anymore.

CHAPTER TEN

The Return

Where does backsliding begin?

"In the knees," some say.

Perhaps. But in a training school for Christian workers?

It is difficult to pinpoint the place where love begins to cool. Even for those who have experienced it. In trying to diagnose the precise moment that his forward motion slowed, Dr. Van Impe finds himself groping. That it happened, he is the first to admit.

And what was the reason for his excursion into no-man's-land?

"Familiarity breeds contempt," he offers, then suggests a number of other possible pitfalls.

Perhaps it was the constant Christian cloister that contributed to his backsliding. It has happened to students in Bible schools before. It is so easy to feel complacent and beyond the line of danger when in a sheltered atmosphere.

Did not even Peter boast that he was spiritually impregnable when in the company of the disciples on the Mount of Olives? Yet, in a few hours he was warming his hands at the devil's fire while cursing and denying his Lord. No wonder Paul warned his Corinthian readers about the danger of overconfidence (I Corinthians 10:12).

On the other hand, the college may have had a tempering effect in the other direction. He states that one sign of his spiritual decline was his neglect of the Bible. He stopped reading it in a devotional manner and exposed himself to the inspired message only when it was necessary to fulfill class assignments. It was just another textbook. Almost.

The Christian who avoids his Bible is certainly on dangerous ground. No one ever gets strong enough to be independent of God's Word. It is both milk and solid food for the soul, and its neglect can only result in spiritual starvation. It was, indeed, a serious mistake to limit all Bible reading to classroom responsibilities.

But what if there had been no assignments? Would the absence of this required study of God's Word have kept his relationship with God more blessed? Can we be sure that spiritual freshness would have continued, and improved, had his exposure to the Bible been more spontaneous? Is victory always sure because its vital ingredients are voluntary? Not at all! Otherwise, there would be no backsliders outside the walls of Christian schools. And they are legion.

There is the possibility, then, that even this rote reading of the Scriptures, poor though it was, may have kept him from going deeper into the far country. Who can tell how distant his wanderings or how severe the necessary chastening had he not been under the influence of godly men and Christian associates? The answer is beyond us. But the obvious conclusion is that some Bible is better than no Bible at all, even when the reading is because of an imposed discipline. It was his knowledge of the Bible that enabled Jack Van Impe to know the route home when his heart was ready to return.

Other signs of backsliding were normal. Sunday church services became unimportant unless he was to participate. Though he would not have been likely to have said it, his actions announced that his contribution to the ministry of any church was more important than that of the pastor. After all, was he not taught daily by some of the most qualified instructors in the Detroit area? Every day was the Lord's Day! He was in church all the time! Why should he not rest when his talents weren't being used? Besides, he might want to use some of that time on his class work and that was all Bible-related.

He began to enjoy the applause at his performances. The genuine joy of service for the Lord's sake became subservient to the thrill of appreciation from the audience. If there was not actual hand-clapping, there were the many "well dones" following the meeting. It was the expected thing. And with his ability, there were always many admirers.

Advertising pieces exalting his musical accomplishments catered to his pride. "Jack Van Impe, the Flying-Fingered Accordionist," was one of his favorites.

One writer from London, Ontario had written to the newspaper that Jack was "out of this world . . . tops, colossal, tremendous, indescribable." It was music to his ears.

The fact that he was constantly in demand as a musician for the top speakers of the day further lifted his ego. Billy Graham, George Beverly Shea, Cliff Barrows and other well-knowns were all his platform associates in Youth For Christ rallies when that movement was at the peak of its strong fundamentalist ministry.

On campus he became "Mr. Comedian." Always ready for a good time, he would now give wrong answers in class just to attract attention. "Smarting off" to other students and even sometimes to instructors began to be a part of his manner. "Off-color" jokes invaded his mind and started to monopolize his conversation with the fellows. It kept him the center of the action.

With his knowledge of the Bible, he should have known that this kind of living would soon bring about divine action—some movement of circumstances to remind him that as a Christian he had all the attention he needed. Reflecting, he remembers that he knew, but quieted the still small voice that kept speaking to him. He had become too cold and indifferent to respond to the gentle moving of God's Spirit, within.

The moment of truth came while on the way to a meeting where he was to play his accordion. He was travelling at 65 m.p.h. in an effort to maintain his reputation for punctuality. Somehow he lost control of the car and it rolled over, landing on its top in a ditch. In a moment he knew the reason. Hebrews

12:6 flashed through his mind: "For whom the Lord loveth he chasteneth, and scourgeth every son whom he receiveth."

He crawled out of the car and looked at the damage. It was a total loss. He remembered how he had stopped tithing some time ago and had used the money to make his car payments, reasoning that it was all right since he was using the automobile in the Lord's work. Now the tithe money was lost as well as much of his own investment, since the insurance was inadequate to cover the loss.

His expensive accordion was inside the overturned car and as he stood there he was unsure of the damage to that instrument so important to him.

He was at the end of himself. Ready to get right with God.

By now, a sizeable crowd had gathered. It was a busy highway and within moments the police had been summoned, and the number of gawkers was increasing steadily. Nevertheless, oblivious to the onlookers, he knelt in the ditch beside the wrecked automobile and confessed his sins to the Lord. Describing the experience he says, "I knew what I had to do, and I did it. I didn't care about those who were watching."

Long before, he had memorized I John 1:9: "If we confess our sins, he is faithful and just to forgive us our sins, and to cleanse us from all unrighteousness." Now its message became personal to him. He felt the release as he claimed God's promise of forgiveness. It was as if a great load had been lifted. He told the Lord he was through backsliding. That he would get back into church, and that he would study the Bible so as to be equipped to give its message to others.

It was not an empty vow. He rose from his knees and has been busy carrying out that road-side promise ever since.

Before making a public announcement of his new commitment he needed some time alone with the Lord in prayer. There were some things to settle about the future. A deepening of his "ditch decision."

Following that, he made an appointment with Dr. Aldrich, the president of the college, and explained all that had happened in his life. He apologized for his attitude and actions and asked for time in chapel to tell the student body what God had done in his life. Dr. Aldrich understood and granted his request.

It was an unusual chapel service. Not an easy one for Jack Van Impe. He had been seeking and enjoying the spotlight. Now he would just as soon have escaped this platform appearance. But again, he knew what he must do!

He began by apologizing for his conduct among the students. He admitted his "smarting off" to both students and teachers. Confessing to circulating "off-color" stories, he asked forgiveness of his classmates. He then told them about his experience by the side of the road and testified to the reality of God's chastening for backsliding, sharing his conversation with the Lord that had taken place in the ditch beside his wrecked car.

He fought back the tears as he pledged publicly his rededication to the Lord and to His service. He urged those who might be in the same spiritual slump that he had experienced, to come back to the Lord immediately.

It is hard to evaluate the impact of this heart-baring by Jack Van Impe before his friends and classmates. There was no surge forward at the end of chapel. No great revival swept the campus as a result of his honest and open confession. We do not know the results, if any, that flowed from his openness. It seems fair, however, to guess that some who might soon have been headed downward were turned about that morning, and that God's work in one young man's heart brought blessing to others who knew him.

Jack had promised the Lord he would study the Bible. He now began to feel that the most effective way to do that was by memorization. Dr. Allen had set an excellent and powerful example and Oscar had left the material to start. Five hundred Bible verses on cards had been left at his house by the Belgian missionary. His son wasn't sure whether they had been left by accident or were part of Oscar's plan to get him into the habit of memorization. No matter, they were there to use, and wonderfully catalogued according to doctrinal truth. He began to use them immediately.

The plan was successful beyond his expectations. He was amazed at how much he could retain by going over and over the verses through the day. He carried several cards with him at all times so he could make good use of every spare minute. He even propped one on the steering wheel of the car so he could work on his memorization while waiting at traffic lights and in the tie-ups that occur in Detroit's work traffic.

Dr. Van Impe still uses this method of memorization and has a stack of cards that stands taller than he, with a number of verses on each card. He now has mastered over eight thousand verses through rigid self-discipline and hard work.

He is quick to admit that the same technique may not work for everyone. His friend Stanley Koenke, for example, tried propping verses on the steering wheel while driving and ran into the back of a truck the very first day. Obviously, he had to change his approach.

The evangelist believes that saturation of the mind with God's Word is the best defense against backsliding. His discovery is not original. It was announced by David long ago: "Thy word have I hid in mine heart, that I might not sin against thee" (Psalm 119:11).

"I am a different man," says Dr. Van Impe, "if I am away from my memorization for even a few days." The constant flow of God's Word through his mind is, without doubt, one of the secrets of his effectiveness for Christ.

With his experience as a prodigal behind him, Jack began again to think of the future. The old desire to excel returned, with a stronger desire than ever that every accomplishment be for the glory of God. He had tasted the bitterness of self-exaltation and wanted nothing more to do with it.

He was ready to serve in whatever way his Lord would use him.

CHAPTER ELEVEN

Say It With Music

For as long as he could remember, Jack Van Impe had longed for the life of a musician. Before he became a Christian, he dreamed of performing on the top stages of the world. After his conversion, he planned for a life of Christian service in music.

Others agreed.

In his youth, his Christian friends urged him to pursue his goal. They were captivated by his natural ability with the accordion, and envisioned him providing the musical spark for great youth rallies and evangelistic crusades.

During high school, playing the accordion for assemblies and special programs made him well-known among the students and furnished openings for witnessing. Music seemed a natural door opener for his Christian testimony. He felt sure it was the way to go.

The summer preceding his first year at D.B.C. had brought the offer to travel with evangelist Leonard Thompson. It was an enviable opportunity, for one his age, and confirmed his convictions about the value of music in the Lord's work. The comments made by people in the congregations that summer encouraged his musical ambition. Some who made decisions credited music as the moving factor in their commitment.

By the time he was eighteen, the young musician had his own professional card. It simply read: "Jack Van Impe. . . . Accordionist." For all he knew, that would be his title for life.

Shortly after beginning his Bible College training, he started

Jack's grandparents,
Mr. and Mrs. Joseph Van Impe

Trip to Belgium L. to R.:
Stanley Koenke, Jack, Louise, Oscar

appearing weekly on television, with Dr. Robert Parr, on "The America Back to God Hour." Dr. Parr was a dynamic preacher and pastor of one of the fastest-growing churches in America. His Sunday School had an attendance of over three thousand and his impact on the Detroit area was considerable. It was through Dr. Parr that Jack met Bob Shelton, a young tenor soloist and T.V. announcer. They became good friends and, next to his conversion, this contact would bring him to the most important experience of his life.

The Voice of Christian Youth (Youth For Christ in Detroit) used Jack's musical talent often. He was the featured musician at a number of their meetings and played his accordion for their great anniversary rallies, gatherings that were packed with outstanding gospel artists.

Youth For Christ contacts kept Jack busy all during his Bible College years. He appeared in rallies both here and in Canada. One newspaper advertisement for a meeting in London, Ontario, featured Billy Graham (billed as: Vice-President of Youth For Christ International; President of Northwestern Schools; the World's Leading Youth Evangelist), with Jack Van Impe as one of the featured musicians. Fifteen hundred free seats were offered.

The great outreach and strong fundamentalist ministry of Youth For Christ, at that time, made it an excellent outlet for Jack's talent and provided a strengthening influence in his life.

A number of well-known evangelists, eager to have competent musical help, offered attractive positions to him if he would leave school and travel with them. The invitations were not easy for a young man to resist, but fortunately, better judgment prevailed and he continued his education to graduation.

Friends of Bible College days agree that Jack avoided speaking responsibilities whenever possible. If an assignment or engagement came that required both music and message, he was quick to take the musical part of the service, leaving the preaching to one of his fellow students.

There were at least two reasons for his reluctance in the pulpit. The first was his belief that his ministry would be in the field of music. He saw little use in practice-preaching when he expected that to be only a minor part of his future work.

The second, and greater reason, probably is found in his perfectionism. He was afraid to preach. He didn't feel he could do an adequate job. Fear of failure was crippling him again. Tying his hands. Limiting his horizons. Had he not finally broken through that stifling characteristic, there would have been no Van Impe world-wide ministry story to tell. His life would have been far less effective.

The most important factor in Dr. Van Impe's liberation from fear, and his ultimate move into preaching, was his decision to start memorizing the Bible. After the close call with the car and his return to close fellowship with his Lord, those Bible memory cards became his constant companions. Though it would take a few years, that regular intake of God's Word finally brought release from his apprehensions about speaking and gave him a large and powerful ministry.

Storing such a great amount of the Bible in his heart produced an experience much like that of the prophet Jeremiah, who wrote: "But his word was in mine heart like a burning fire shut up in my bones, and I was weary with forbearing, and I could not stay" (Jeremiah 20:9).

By the last semester of his senior year at Detroit Bible College, evidence was starting to show that preaching would be an important part of his life. Still expecting a major share of his work to be in music, he began to see his accordion playing as a valuable tool to bring people together so that he could preach to them. As a result, he requested ordination to the gospel ministry.

Jack Van Impe's ordination council gathered at the Christian Fellowship Tabernacle at Marine City, Michigan, on March 26, 1951. The examining council was composed of eleven ministers. They were: Dr. A.G. Kruschwitz, Rev. Earl Linderholm, Dr. W.S. Hottel, Rev. L.P. Buroker, Rev. Albert Ludwig, Rev. John Pinches, Rev. Harry E. Cochenour, Rev. Orrin Van Loon, Sr., Rev. Orrin Van Loon, Jr., Rev. Harold Moran, and Rev. William Reiter. The chairman of the council was Dr. W.S. Hottel, a noted Bible teacher and writer.

Though lacking experience, the young minister's work in Bible memorization had prepared him well for his ordination examination. The verses his father left behind had been categorized as to doctrine and Jack had mastered all of them. With the doctrinal foundation of over five hundred verses, he laid out his beliefs to the examining body. Notes were used for stating the doctrines, but all the Bible verses on which the doctrines are built were given, in machine-gun fashion, from memory. The older men were immediately aware of the discipline and hard work involved in preparation for the examination and reacted favorably. Their action may be unprecedented.

The *Fundamental Fellowship*, a Michigan religious periodical, in reporting the ordination headed their article: "Jack Van Impe Ordained to Ministry Following Unusual Ordination Council." The subtitle read: "Only One Question Asked Following Doctrinal Statement."

So thorough was the young candidate's coverage of Bible doctrine that the seasoned men thought only one question necessary. Dr. Hottel, the chairman of the council, voiced it: "Jack, do you really believe what you have just told us you believe?" With no hesitation, Jack replied: "Yes, sir, I certainly do, with all my heart."

"Gentlemen," said Dr. Hottel, "we have another Martin Luther on our hands. Let's ordain him."

The council voted unanimously to dispense with the customary questioning and to recommend that the Marine City congregation proceed with the ordination.

That news article contains a significant paragraph about Jack Van Impe's life and future. That April 8, 1951 issue of The *Fundamental Fellowship* reported: "Mr. Van Impe is widely known as an accordionist, having maintained a heavy schedule of engagements in churches and in youth meetings. He told the council that there was a time when he felt that he could be perfectly happy in the Lord's work with his accordion, but that in recent months he had learned that his testimony and musical work were not enough, that he had found himself under obligation 'to preach the Word'."

The tide was turning. A preacher was being prepared.

The service of ordination was held that evening. It was described as follows:

Those participating in the service of consecration were: Dr. Kruschwitz, who presided; Rev. Linderholm, who presented the report of the ordination council and prayed; Dr. Hottel, who gave the charge to Mr. Van Impe; Rev. L. P. Buroker, editor of The *Fundamental Fellowship*, who gave the charge to the people; Rev. Albert Ludwig, missionary to Haiti, who read the Scripture; Rev. John Pinches, of the Emmanual Bible Church, Detroit, who preached the sermon; Rev. Harry E. Cochenour, of the Gethsemane Baptist Church, Detroit, who offered the prayer of ordination; and Rev. Van Impe, who led the singing, presented two numbers on his accordion and pronounced the benediction.

A vocal duet by Mrs. Linderholm, wife of the St. Clair pastor, and their daughter was a part of the service.

It was now official. The call of God to His servant, Jack Van Impe, had been recognized by men of God and by the church. The wisdom of that public recognition would be demonstrated to the world in years to come.

When, a short time later, Detroit Bible College graduated Rev. Jack Van Impe, he had accepted the fact that an important part of his ministry would be preaching the Word of God. Now, the fear of preaching had about vanished. His "A" average at graduation testified to the quality of his preparation from an academic standpoint, but he had gone far beyond the requirements of the school in equipping himself for his life's work.

And that "extra equipping" made the difference. Those 500 Bible verses he had committed to memory were showing up in his sermons. Over the years, that characteristic of his preaching would become his trademark, and the power of "The Word" would propel his ministry around the world.

Following graduation from D.B.C., Jack and his friend, Stanley Koenke, departed for Belgium to do missionary work with

Oscar and Louise. They were sent by Youth For Christ as European Team number 102. The two had been preparing for the trip during the school year and were eager to serve the Lord on foreign soil. They had visited churches and solicited the support of friends to make the journey possible.

The young missionaries sailed for Belgium on the R.M.S. Nieuw Amsterdam, a large, impressive ship that crossed the Atlantic in ten days. It was their first experience aboard an ocean liner and they boarded with excitement. The size of the vessel was almost overwhelming and it seemed there were a thousand things to see. The trip was a college graduate's dream. And, besides the intrigue and adventure, they were serving the Lord.

True to his pattern, Jack practiced his accordion from three to four hours daily on the voyage. He wanted to be at his best in the Belgian work, especially while working with his father and in the presence of his relatives.

The professional-sounding music coming from his room caught the ear of one of the ship's officers, who asked him to present a concert for the passengers. Jack wrestled with the invitation for a time, since the concert was to be given in the ballroom, a setting that reminded him all too much of his night club experiences. Nevertheless, he decided it was an unusual opportunity to witness to the 2,000 passengers on the Nieuw Amsterdam, and he finally accepted.

The program, when settled upon, called for three concerts, one for each class aboard. Jack played a variety of good music, including several marches, and then moved into gospel music. When the mood was right, he shared the testimony of God's work in his family. He told of their night club entertaining, the drinking, the emptiness of it all, and described the miracle of their conversion. And all this to an audience made up of people sitting at tables in a ballroom, many of which were topped with drinks.

Following one of the concerts, a young lady asked for more information about the wonderful change that had taken place in

Jack's family. He and Stanley were able to open the Scriptures with her and lead her to Christ. His self-discipline in practicing had borne fruit beyond his expectations.

Having discovered that he was a minister, the proper powers on the ship asked if he would like to preach for the Protestant services on Sunday. Without hesitation, he accepted and ministered to nearly four hundred people. It was a great opportunity to share the Word of God with the other passengers. This was really a missionary journey.

Up to this time, Jack had never seen a relative other than his parents. Now, with Oscar and Louise serving the Lord in Belgium, every living member of his family awaited his arrival in that country.

Oscar had written that the entire welcoming group would be gathered at Rotterdam to greet them. He had arranged a signal by which Jack and Stan could recognize them, even at a distance. "We'll have both the Belgian and American flags," he had explained. "When you see those two flags, you'll know it's your family."

On the morning of the scheduled arrival, the two travelers were up extra early, straining their eyes for the shore and looking for those flying flags. Remembering the occasion makes Dr. Van Impe think about what heaven must be like. When the flags were in sight, the anticipation was exhilarating.

As they disembarked from the ship, there was a glad reunion with Jack's parents and a wonderful meeting with his relatives. The hugs and handshakes, the tears and laughter, were indeed heavenly, and the scene was much like one to come on another shore.

The missionary work of Oscar and Louise had been fruitful. A number of the family had been saved and were serving the Lord. A new church had been started. The newlyweds who had departed their native land and returned with the Good News were seeing the results of their labor. Prayers were being answered. The investment of missionary dollars had been more than worthwhile; the dividends would be eternal.

The summer was a busy one. Oscar and Jack attracted

crowds in the streets of Belgium's cities with their excellent and lively accordion music. When a sufficient number had gathered, Oscar and Jack gave their testimonies, while Stanley distributed tracts. Usually, Oscar brought a Bible message.

It was a pattern repeated effectively, again and again. Sometimes there was visible fruit. Other days were discouraging. Regardless of the results, however, they stayed at it, knowing they had been called of God to be faithful.

The Van Impe missionary work in Belgium has been a lasting ministry. Today, twenty-five years after Jack and Stanley visited that country, the work continues. One member of the family, Rev. Albert Trippaers (Dr. Van Impe's cousin), is on the staff of Jack Van Impe Crusades as a full-time missionary. He and his wife, Gayle, carry on an intense and extensive evangelistic work there.

As the three months of missionary work in Belgium drew to a close, Jack had mixed feelings. He was thrilled with the work of God in members of his family and others, and his heart was burdened by the great need in that land. It would have been easy to consider that overwhelming need his call to stay and serve the Lord. Still, deep in his heart, there was the pull of America. A sense that his ministry must begin there.

Parting was again tearful as Jack and Stanley departed their summer mission field. Jack found it difficult to leave his family again. Yet, there was an undeniable anticipation of the future. Engagements already scheduled for the fall would make good use of his musical talent.

Stepping off European soil and boarding the ship, the two young men waved to those with whom they had labored for the past three months. It had been a wonderful summer—one they would never forget.

As the ocean liner headed out into the Atlantic, it moved Jack Van Impe toward the most important meeting of his entire ministry. There he would meet a talented and attractive young soprano soloist. They would fall in love and make beautiful music together.

Jack and Rosella at their wedding

CHAPTER TWELVE

Finding A Wife

Rev. Jack Van Impe may have been moving close to a decision to major in preaching, but to the Youth For Christ organization, he was "Jack Van Impe, Accordionist Supreme." That is the way he was billed for the Pontiac Youth For Christ Rally in October, 1951. Also on the program was soloist Rexella Shelton.

Like the accordionist, Rexella was no stranger to the platform. She and her brother, Bob, had been singing together since they were small children. Having grown up in the large and active First Baptist Church of Pontiac, Michigan, she was at ease singing before large audiences. She had also been involved in music during her high school years. An article in the newspaper at that time announced that she had captured vocal honors at the University of Michigan solo and ensemble festival.

An accomplished pianist, she knew both the vocal and instrumental fields of Christian music. In addition to her involvement in the musical ministry of her church, she had studied in that field at Bob Jones University in Greenville, South Carolina.

Praying for a wife was a rather steady occupation for young Rev. Van Impe in those days. He recalls he was doing just that while waiting his slot in the program that evening, when he heard soft footsteps and looked up to see Rexella Shelton headed for the center of the stage. He knew in a moment his prayers had been answered.

He listened with rapt attention as she communicated the gospel song to the youthful crowd and explained in her testimony that she felt God was calling her to some work in evangelism. When she turned to go back to her place on the platform, her eyes met his. His earlier reaction was confirmed. It was one of those rare experiences of love at first sight.

There was one problem. She was dating another fellow.

Dr. Van Impe has delighted crusade audiences across the nation with the story of his capture of Rexella. The Bible says "Watch and pray," he says. "So, that's what I did! I watched them both and prayed the Lord would remove the other fellow."

Following that Pontiac rally, Bob Shelton, Jack's friend from "The America Back To God Hour," introduced him to Rexella. It was the beginning of an intense co-operative effort by these two young men. Bob felt that Jack was the man for his sister and used his influence to aid the ardent accordionist.

The chase was on.

Rexella Shelton was seldom off Jack's mind during the next few months. He kept reliving that magic moment on the platform at the rally. His prayer life flourished as he enlisted all available resources to move that other fellow, his only obstacle, out of the way.

Faithful brother Bob kept plotting and praying, also. He invited Jack to their home to visit. Quite normal for such fast friends, but in this case the object was to get his sister better acquainted with her suitor.

Another valuable member was added to the Van Impe team when Rexella's father began to voice his approval of the promising young preacher-musician. Rex Shelton liked Jack from the start and saw him as excellent husband material for the apple of his eye.

Rexella, meanwhile, was enjoying the pursuit. She had been impressed at that first formal meeting with the Y.F.C. accordionist, but wasn't about to let it be known. Being aware of the young musician's reputation as a zealous Christian, and having heard him play his accordion at her church, she was delighted at the opportunity of getting to know him personally. Now that his romantic interests were evident, she basked in the attention awhile before giving him any real encouragement.

It was December before Rexella officially stopped dating the "other fellow." She had been praying earnestly about God's will for her life and became convinced he was not the man she should marry. She kindly explained this to him and let her family know about her decision.

Her father welcomed this opening for his favored future son-in-law, but it was Bob who made the major move. He invited Rexella to sing on "The America Back To God Hour," knowing that Jack would be playing his accordion on the same telecast.

Waiting in the wings at the television studio, Rexella listened to the musical ministry of the young man who now had become her favorite accordionist. During those few moments she was engaged in a brief conversation by Stanley Koenke, another member of the "Get Rexella Squad."

"Are you still dating that guy?" Stan asked.

"No, I'm not," she answered softly.

"Oh, Jack's going to be happy to hear that!" Stan exclaimed.

Her heart did a light flip at his reaction, but her face was expressionless. She was outwardly calm. Unmoved.

A few days after the telecast, Jack called to ask Rexella for their first date. She accepted, and they attended a youth rally together. It was the Christmas season of 1951.

The early months of 1952 were busy and exciting for the young evangelist-musician. Speaking opportunities were opening, as his reputation became known, and the calls for his music seemed unending. Between meetings he cultivated the courtship with Rexella. When they were apart, letters carried their messages of young love. It was great to be alive.

Bob, who had been so helpful in promoting their romance, now became somewhat of an obstacle. Though still convinced his friend was the man for Rexella, he felt a responsibility as her older brother to be her protector. In those first months, he accompanied them on all dates. The presence of this third party was a bit stifling to the amorous accordionist so he began praying about his problem.

Soon, brother Bob's missionary support came in and he headed for Formosa to preach the gospel. Dr. Van Impe still jokes with his brother-in-law about how long it might have taken him to work up to a prosposal had the Formosan field not called.

Toward the end of February, the youthful evangelist set out for Filion, Michigan to hold his first full-length evangelistic crusade. He had been preaching here and there in one-night or week end meetings and had provided music for other speakers, but this was the real opener. The five nights in Filion would be the forerunner of city-wide crusades and a world-wide outreach. Neither the little congregation nor the evangelist suspected they were launching such a ministry.

The tiny Filion Gospel Church was a challenge to optimism, to say the least. The building was heated with a pot-bellied stove that was fired only an hour before the time of the service. Michigan winters do not tame easily, and often the congregation shivered through the sermons.

Their young evangelist, however, had been there hours before the fire was started. Still faithful to his schedule of daily practice on the accordion, he arrived at the church every afternoon to exercise his flying fingers and to perfect his musical presentation. It was a trying experience, but the faithful minister maintained his self-discipline and endured. That kind of determination has carried him through many difficult situations in his later ministry.

Chilling as the conditions were, they did not shake him as much as the thought of his final night there. Five nights of meetings were scheduled and at that point in his ministry he had only mastered four sermons. He prayed fervently that the Lord would give him one more message before the end of the crusade.

Finally, feeling directed to a printed sermon by evangelist Dr. John R. Rice, he adapted it for his closing service. It seemed to be just what the congregation needed, and the crusade ended with mild success. He was on his way.

Driving back from Filion, the tired but excited preacher thought seriously about the young lady God had brought into his life. He had dated many girls during his high school and Bible College years, but none like this one. She was everything he wanted. Her beauty ran deep. Her warm blue eyes made him feel at ease. And when they were apart, he longed to be with her.

Most important, they were spiritually compatible. Both in love with Christ. Eager to serve. He decided it was time to intensify his efforts. He would tell her of his love and ask her to be his bride.

It wasn't long after the Filion Crusade that Jack and Rexella had one of their most significant dates. They went to a service at the North Detroit Baptist Church, where the Van Impes' former pastor, Dr. John Hunter, was now the minister. He had invited Jack to preach in the Sunday evening service.

Rexella listened as her young preacher friend unfolded his message that evening. She was moved, as she still is, by the evidence of God's hand on him, and was pleased that their ways had met. She felt close to him and wondered about their future.

Both the Van Impes especially remember that night. It seems to have been a turning point in their relationship. From here on, every happy step would lead them closer to the marriage altar.

Now that he had developed a full week's supply of sermons, doors began to open for a number of church crusades. In spite of his youth, seasoned ministers called on him to hold meetings in their churches. They knew they could be sure of an outstanding musical program, a feature that increased attendance, and that he would give their congregations plenty of Bible. That combination made him acceptable to many preachers and as a result he was away from his home area a considerable amount of time. A difficult situation for a young man in love.

On the few nights he was able to see Rexella, he remembers he had to be careful not to keep her out late nor linger too long at her door. A late hour was sure to bring the raising and lowering of the Shelton windows. That was Rexella's mother's signal that it was time to come in. Preacher-suitor or not, Esther Shelton's disciplines remained rigid. She had produced a fine young lady with these rules and she wasn't about to change them just because she was dating an evangelist.

Both Jack and Rexella look back thankfully at the consistency of discipline carried out by their parents.

The courtship of these two young lovers was a relationship built around spiritual things. Most of their dates were to services where he was preaching and where she gave musical numbers, either vocally or on the piano. They always prayed together at some time during an evening out. When they were apart, their letters were filled with love and conversation about the ministry and their future. They were happy and there was always lots of joking and fun.

When June of 1952 arrived, Jack felt it was time to propose. He was sure Rexella was the girl God intended for him to marry and he could see no reason for further delay. Enlisting the experience of his friend, Dr. Parr, he went diamond hunting.

On a warm summer evening in June, Rexella Shelton was asked to become Mrs. Jack Van Impe. They had attended a prayer meeting and found the house empty when they arrived home. The moon was shining into the large picture window and Jack saw the setting as ideal for his important question.

Taking Rexella's hand and leading her near the window, he said, "I remember your testimony at the Youth Rally, where we met, about your call to evangelistic work. Would you join me in a lifetime partnership, serving the Lord together? I'd like to have you for my wife." With that heartfelt proposal, he took the ring from his pocket and offered it to her. "I love you Jack," she answered softly, "and I'll accept your ring tonight, but tomorrow you must get the approval of my parents."

Her answer was all he had hoped for. He knew her respect for her family and had expected the condition she had tied to her acceptance. No matter. He knew that God had given him this lovely girl, and was confident of her parents' consent.

It was a wonderful and unforgettable moment. He walked out into the pleasant moonlight, a happy man. In a few months, Rexella would be his wife.

After Rex and Esther Shelton had given their approval, the wedding date was set for August 21. Needless to say, those few months were busy ones. All the usual responsibilities were made especially heavy because of the groom's schedule. Even so, when the day arrived, everything moved with precision. Rexella and her mother had cared for every detail.

Jack was delighted with the eight hundred guests who came to the wedding and personally greeted each one at the door of the church. As he thinks back on the occasion, he says that he welcomed everyone as if they were coming to a revival meeting. He had but one regret: his parents were still in Belgium and unable to attend.

The marriage ceremony was performed at the First Baptist Church of Pontiac, Michigan, by Rev. H.H. Savage, Rexella's pastor. Nancy Harrison came from South Bend, Indiana to be her maid of honor. Bridesmaids were Eleanor Billingsley, Wilma Pickering, and Vonnie Whitten. Becky Sue Brown and Judy Gidley were flower girls.

Jack's close friend, Stanley Koenke, was the best man and usher's duties were performed by Donald Shelton, David Hunter (Dr. John Hunter's son), and Rev. Gordon Lindsay.

It was a great day. A beautiful wedding. The beginning of a wonderful marriage. The deep and lasting things that happened on that occasion are locked in the hearts of the two people who became one at 8 p.m., August 21, 1952.

At the reception, the groom played his accordion and gave his personal testimony. They wanted their wedding and reception to carry the message that would be the center of their lives and the purpose of their existence.

The next day the newlyweds departed for Mackinac Island, a beautiful resort near the straits of Mackinac, in Michigan. The first night of their trip they stopped at a Bible conference at

Traverse City, a picturesque place on the shore of Lake Michigan. Jack was to speak there on Saturday night at a youth rally before proceeding to their honeymoon destination.

Following the Saturday night rally, the honeymooners were prevailed upon to remain another day. Since it would be Sunday, and they wanted to attend church services somewhere, anyway, they consented. Sunday brought another plea to remain the next day and assist in the meetings, for which they would be furnished a lovely lakeside cottage and given total privacy. Again, they accepted, and moved "temporarily" into the cottage.

At five a.m. on Monday, the speaker for the week (Dr. John Zoller) knocked at the cottage door and asked the honeymooning preacher if he would like to go fishing. Their privacy was not quite total.

The Van Impes never made it to Mackinac Island. They spent the entire week playing, singing, and speaking in the services at the Bible conference.

On the surface, it seems sad that their honeymoon plans were not fulfilled, but perhaps it is significant. Their experience that week gave a preview of their life together.

And the honeymoon continues.

CHAPTER THIRTEEN

On The Road

There's something romantic about the thought of a life of evangelism. The travel, the appreciation of different congregations, the limelight, the glory, final nights with great public response, and other common conceptions about this divine calling make it an intriguing occupation.

Having grown up in an era blessed with an abundance of these prophets of the open road, Rev. and Mrs. Jack Van Impe viewed their future in that field a bit starry-eyed. Though Jack had done some summer travelling and had been busy furnishing music for other evangelists, besides holding crusades of his own, the two young Christian workers had no real understanding of the grind of constant meetings year in and year out.

After getting comfortably settled in the Van Impe home on Liberal Avenue (now rented from Oscar and Louise, who were on the mission field), they set out for their first crusade together, in Bay City, Michigan. Since they were equipped to provide both music and the message in their meetings, they had decided to travel under a name they hoped would convey the image of a team. They called themselves "Ambassadors For Christ."

It was a good title, being both biblical and descriptive, but it never really caught on with the public. In Bay City, and across the nation, they would be known affectionately as "Jack and Rexella."

That first crusade set a pattern that developed again and

again through the years. The warm-hearted, sincere, approach of these two talented young people captured the hearts of those in the local congregation and the size of the crowd increased throughout the week. Rexella sang nightly and Jack conveyed his enthusiasm for life and the gospel through the accordion. His sermons were loaded with Bible verses and delivered in a fiery evangelistic manner that demanded attention and produced results.

Dr. Van Impe still marvels over the public response to their ministry in those early years. "We were so young," he says, "yet people accepted us and the meetings kept growing."

There were reasons for that acceptance and enthusiasm. Both he and Rexella demanded excellence of themselves without yielding to professionalism. They were human and happy enough for people to take them to their hearts. Nothing fake at all. They had come to serve the Lord. To win souls. To revive the church. Their listeners understood and spread the word. The results were predictable. The blessing of the Lord was upon their efforts.

Rexella says the first year in evangelism was a great learning experience. Her education started in Bay City. For the next twelve years she and her husband would live the greater share of their lives in the homes of others. On the first night of that nomadic existence, she felt insecure and insisted that Jack pile the bedroom furniture in front of the door so no one could break into their room. Obediently, the young husband moved a number of the heavy items in the room into place, making a barricade to intruders so Rexella could sleep safely. It would have been a relatively harmless case of female fear had not Jack become ill in the night and needed to exit the room in a hurry. All the furniture had to be moved in haste before the "upset evangelist" could get out of their well-fortified quarters. Rexella has never again demanded such tight security.

Staying in private homes does present problems. In order to avoid the "professional evangelist" image, the Van Impes ad-

vised their hosts against motel accommodations and requested
lodging in homes for the first twelve years of their ministry. As
might be expected, they often suffered from lack of needed
privacy.

Being young and full of fun, they usually had conversations
long into the night about humorous and interesting things that
had happened during the day. This necessitated whispering,
and laughing in hushed tones, so as not to disturb others in the
house. They became so accustomed to this stifling of sound that
one day they found themselves conversing in whispers as they
went about their work at their own home. The need for a more
normal existence finally led them to accept arrangements for
staying in motels.

Following the Bay City Crusade, other openings in music and
evangelism kept the young couple busy. About half their time
was spent conducting their own meetings with the remainder
being used to provide music for other evangelists and at special
rallies.

Since Rexella had never met her husband's parents, they
began planning a trip to Belgium. It seemed a wonderful opportunity to get the whole family together and offered valuable
experience in missionary work, while aiding Oscar and Louise
in their ministry. Three months in the summer of 1953 were set
aside for the European journey.

The Reverend Dick Robinson of Atlantic City, New Jersey,
had invited them to hold a seventeen-day crusade at his church
and the timing was such that after finishing the meetings there
they could leave for Belgium. It all seemed to fit so well into
their schedule that they felt sure it was in the Lord's will and
arranged their other meetings accordingly.

The Van Impes departed from Hoboken, New Jersey on the
"Maasdam" for a ten-day crossing to Belgium. For Rexella, it
seemed like an eternity. She was seasick all the way. In spite of
her discomfort, however, they were able to serve the Lord.
Getting acquainted with a missionary couple on board, they

worked together in a number of gospel meetings on the ship. Again, Jack was able to share his testimony with the passengers and use the trip itself as a means of missionary work.

Flags were flying when Jack and Rexella arrived in Rotterdam.

There, as before, the Van Impe family was waiting, holding the Belgian and American flags. It was another glad reunion for Jack and his parents and a special occasion as he introduced Rexella to all the relatives. Oscar and Louise were overjoyed at their son's choice of a wife and recognized immediately that God had arranged this marriage. They saw their attractive daughter-in-law as an answer to their prayers.

In getting acquainted with her husband's family, Rexella came to an understanding of the forces that had shaped the man she loved. Oscar's boundless enthusiasm and Louise's quiet nature seemed so perfectly blended in their son. She was grateful for the opportunity of meeting and getting to know them in this setting. It allowed her to reach back to Jack's roots—to feel more a part of him, and to gain a deeper insight into his personality. Her acceptance by the entire family meant much to her and the whole experience confirmed again the direction of the Lord in their lives.

In addition to assisting Jack's parents in their missionary work in Belgium, Jack and Rexella accompanied them on a tour of a number of European countries. The two couples visited France, Holland, Spain, Italy, Switzerland, and Germany.

The excursion was relaxing and enjoyable for the tired missionaries, and gave the younger Van Impes a vision of the spiritual hunger of Europeans. The concern generated on that trip has never left them, and is, in part, responsible for their burden to carry the gospel to the entire world by all means possible.

Jack and Rexella celebrated their first wedding anniversary aboard ship on their return to America. It had been an eventful year. A year of love and learning. A foundation had been established for a lifetime ministry. Convictions were beginning to solidify. Their names were becoming known in an ever-widening area. They were returning to an increasingly busy schedule of music and crusade work.

Arriving home meant being on the road again. Youth For Christ was still one of their most important contacts for meetings. Jack was being used in giant rallies as the featured musician. A number of celebrities had been converted, in those years, who were being promoted on Y.F.C. platforms as speakers. The big name was all-important, but good music rounded out a program. Jack Van Impe, their number one accordionist, was often called to meet that need.

Bible conferences were also eager for quality musicians. Jack was used in a number of them to complement the ministries of well-known Bible teachers. The program for Odosagih Bible Conference in Machias, New York, in 1954, boasted as speakers: Dr. L. Sale Harrison, Dr. Lehman Strauss, Dr. Kenneth Masteller, Dr. Harry Vom Bruch, Dr. Ralph Davis, with Jack Van Impe as the musician. The program brochure announced him as "The Nation's No. 1 Gospel Accordionist."

The Summer Bible Conference of the First Baptist Church of Atlantic City, New Jersey, used Rev. Van Impe for both music and preaching. The copy accompanying his picture in the conference advertising explained: "Jack is not only a fine youth evangelist but also the nation's number 1 gospel accordionist. He and his wife have been in Belgium doing missionary work."

Jack was beginning to mature as a preacher. It was less difficult for him to minister the Word than in the past, though not all his fears were gone. He was still somewhat self-conscious.

One night a well-known pastor attended one of his meetings and the young evangelist became so rattled that, in preaching on the return of the prodigal son, he had the father calling for the servants to come and place shoes on his hands and a ring on his feet.

On another occasion, in relating his own return from backsliding as a result of the automobile accident, he described the scene of the overturned car with his expensive instrument inside and shouted: "There was the car inside the accordion!"

There are many things that go on inside a preacher of which his public is unaware. A necessary fact, because a minister of the gospel who had no private relationship with God would have only a superficial message. A look at the lives of the men God used in Bible times reveals experiences of travail of soul and seasons of deep struggle within.

Moses was only ready to deliver his people after forty years on the backside of the desert, having failed to save them while a prince in Egypt. Paul needed time alone in Arabia. Elijah heard the still, small voice of God only after exposure to the wind, the fire, and the earthquake. Jack Van Impe endured a struggle over a period of years that called for a choice between his first love, music, and the call of God to major in preaching the gospel.

The difficult dimension to this contest over which should come first, the musician or the preacher, was that even during his struggle he seemed to be blending the two abilities into one useful ministry. Reason called for both to continue. What difference did it make which one reigned over the other?

Had it not been for the clear leading of His Lord, Jack Van Impe might never have come to a solid decision on what turned out to be a life-changing issue. But, God is faithful and reveals His will to all who really desire it.

The first step in settling this important issue came, strangely enough, in the form of an invitation to play his accordion at a large gathering of Christian musicians in Pasadena, California. Phil Kerr, of "Monday Night Musicale" fame, had planned a great banquet involving twenty-five hundred musicians from across the nation. Jack Van Impe was to be the featured soloist.

Jack was delighted at receiving the invitation, and accepted. The thought even crossed his mind that this might be God's way of showing him that he belonged in a musical ministry. It appeared to be one of his greatest opportunities.

The celebrated occasion turned out to be a disaster. At the very height of the program, when Jack was at center stage playing "Wonderful Grace of Jesus," the middle C-sharp key fell off his accordion and landed on the floor at his feet.

The musician, so given to perfection in his work, stood horrified and visibly shaken. Unable to continue he called, "Mr. Kerr, Mr. Kerr, the C-sharp has fallen off my accordion!"

"What do you want me to do about it?" Kerr asked. "Shall I hold it on so you can finish?"

The guests roared with applause and laughter. They thought the whole thing was planned as a joke. But it was a serious moment for their featured soloist and he left the banquet in humiliation.

A few months later, Phil Kerr decided to try again. He recognized the talent of the young accordionist and wanted to use him in his "Monday Night Musicale." So, once again, he extended an invitation. Eager to vindicate himself, Jack accepted and arranged his schedule so he could be in Pasadena for the engagement.

A few days before he was to leave for Pasadena, Jack and Rexella were visiting a friend, Rev. Joe Sherman, at Centerville, California.

They had just gathered at the dinner table when, before the meal started, Jack reached for an olive.

Joe kiddingly raised a carving knife and pointed it at Jack's outreached hand, saying: "Hey, we haven't prayed yet!"

Jack reacted to the move with the knife and in his reflex brought his hand directly into the path of the moving knife, cutting his finger deeply.

He was hurried to the hospital and treated. Fortunately the finger, though cut severely, was not permanently injured. The Kerr engagement, however, was out of the question, and the opportunity at Pasadena ended forever.

To some, the two disappointments might seem no more than coincidental. Bad luck. A warning to turn down all Phil Kerr invitations. Even to avoid the city of Pasadena. But Jack Van Impe knew the meaning of those never-to-be-forgotten experiences. God had been speaking to him about making his preaching ministry the most important part of his work. He got the message. That very night, he made a covenant with his Lord that he would not accept invitations only to play the accordion.

All future engagements would have to include the opportunity to preach the gospel.

When he made his decision known, some of his friends were upset. They correctly concluded that many great meetings would be closed to him. The Youth For Christ invitations would end. Well-known evangelists would not be able to use him. His ministry seemed sure to be curtailed. Nevertheless, he knew the decision was right and that he was acting obediently, even if it meant smaller crowds and a limited ministry.

For the next few years the predictions of his friends proved true. The large platforms were closed to him. No matter. Small churches were looking for evangelistic teams like Jack and Rexella and doors continued to open for them. They accepted the humblest places as their special field of service and gave of themselves unreservedly. And God blessed them.

Small churches were packed to capacity time and again. Revival came in out-of-the-way places. Churches sometimes had as many conversions as they had members.

The die was cast. Jack Van Impe would major in the preaching of God's word. They would use their musical talent to help build the crowds, but Jack would never come to any church only to play the accordion. Their future would rest on the effectiveness of a ministry saturated with the Bible.

Slowly, the "accordionist" reputation began to fade. Surprisingly, Jack was glad to see it go.

Instead, churches around the nation began to hear of a young husband and wife evangelistic team that packed church buildings with hungry-hearted people and left solid conversions in the wake of their meetings.

There was no longer any doubt about it. The God of Heaven had called Jack Van Impe to do the work of an evangelist.

CHAPTER FOURTEEN

The Work Of An Evangelist

With the loss of the large meetings and influential contacts, because of his decision to insist on preaching wherever he played the accordion, Jack found the road long and demanding. He and Rexella had agreed to go anywhere the Lord directed them and their openness took them to small and average-sized churches both in large cities and in rural out-of-the-way places.

They logged hundreds of thousands of miles on automobiles, while crisscrossing the country, and many times the offerings barely paid their traveling expenses. One eight-week stint in California brought in only an average of ten dollars per week after paying transportation costs.

Having purchased a small home in Royal Oak, Michigan, they felt the financial pressure of maintaining a home while living most of the time on the road. Days between meetings sometimes found them too far from home to return, adding a greater burden to their already-tight budget.

Dr. Van Impe gives his wife great credit for their happiness and ability to survive financially during those years. He says she was always willing to sacrifice and do without new things to lessen pressures. She kept encouraging him, as they trusted the Lord to meet their needs.

Though the schedule seldom permitted it, there were occasions when the struggling evangelist took secular jobs to help pay their bills. Always ambitious, he sometimes worked as a

Jack and Rexella

painter and once applied to the post office for a position as a mail carrier during the busy holiday season, a time of the year when meetings were usually scarce. "I don't believe in sitting around and claiming I'm waiting for the Lord to provide," he says. Quoting Paul, he adds: "If a man will not work, let him not eat" (II Thess. 3:10).

Even though preaching was now his first responsibility, Jack continued to practice the accordion for at least two hours each day. As he had explained to the pastors at his ordination, music was a useful tool to attract a crowd so that he could preach the gospel to a greater number of people.

Memorization also continued. Those cards filled with Bible verses were with him on every evangelistic tour. He worked on them for a minimum of two hours daily and added extra time while doing other things, when it was possible. Sometimes Rexella assisted him by drilling over verses he had learned. He was determined to be, first and foremost, a man of the Word.

Early in his ministry, Jack settled on his policy concerning the public invitation given at the end of evangelistic services.

He knew there were gimmicks and tricks, used by many preachers, designed to get as many people as possible to come forward. Some of these methods bordered on dishonesty and his heart wouldn't allow him to employ them. He concluded that his invitation to the lost and backslidden would be straightforward and easy to understand, with no traps for his listeners. He wanted decisions and public professions as much as anyone, but was not willing to use carnal means to get them. Convinced that the real results of a meeting are recorded in heaven, he has held to an honest and open invitation and the Lord has rewarded him with many souls. Pastors across the country have learned they can trust him to handle this sensitive part of a meeting with reverence and good taste.

Being faithful to the fundamentals, both biblically and ethically, began to produce results. Churches invited the Van Impes back again and again. New and lasting friendships were formed with ministers and laymen. The power of strong Bible preaching became evident in a number of places.

In a church in Richmond, California, revival came as the youth of the church stayed on their knees in prayer until midnight each night of the crusade. During that week, there were 102 conversions. Beryl Smith, later associated with Dr. Van Impe in evangelism, and his brother Charles, also in Christian work, met Christ in those meetings.

One Michigan pastor scheduled the Van Impes for a crusade and was both startled and overjoyed when half of his membership came forward to be saved, on the first Sunday morning of the meetings. Another church in that area was revolutionized by the conversion of the five deacons who made up the entire church board.

Revival broke out in a Detroit church were Jack was speaking in Sunday School. There was such an evident work of God among the people that the invitation given at the end of Sunday School continued on through the morning service. Scores were saved and about 80 percent of the congregation made significant spiritual decisions.

Not all meetings were mountaintop experiences. Some churches were poorly prepared. There were times when advertising had been so minimal that the greater share of the community wasn't even aware that the crusade was scheduled. Proper prayer support was often lacking. Crusades were sometimes planned just because it was time for the annual revival, or because the denomination called for it. In these cases there was generally little effort put forth by the membership of the church and cooperation by the pastor was less than enthusiastic.

On occasion, God overruled the lethargy of a church or pastor and brought blessing in spite of them. In one such "required revival," the messages immediately penetrated the hearts of the people and on the first week night thirty-five members of the congregation came to the Lord. Though the crusade had been planned as an exercise in formality, it turned into an experience of fire and faith. Oddly enough, the pastor somehow missed the blessing, and when Jack and Rexella arrived at the parsonage, after counselling the converts by themselves, they found the leader of the flock watching television and enjoying pop and potato chips. He and his wife had left the church almost immediately after the service.

Since preachers are people, it isn't strange that some are less spiritual than others.

Upon arriving for a crusade in one church, the Van Impes were advised by a member that if the pastor invited them to play ping pong it would be best to allow him to win. They thought the information was just idle talk and when the pastor's ping pong proposal came they accepted enthusiastically. But, the layman's warning was born out of experience. Rexella beat the pastor in the game and he wouldn't speak to her for the remainder of the week.

A few pastors have tried to tell Rev. Van Impe what to preach.

One minister called Jack on Saturday afternoon, before his message containing his personal testimony, and urged him not to preach on worldliness. "If you do," the preacher said, "everyone will think we're squares."

That night, when Jack brought his message on worldliness, the pastor's daughter was the first to come forward. Also in that service, a doctor was saved, and immediately wrote a sizeable check to the church building fund, a project close to the pastor's heart. It was a worthwhile lesson for the troubled preacher who had been so concerned about the reaction of the community.

A California pastor took Jack aside and said: "Look, I am an older man in the ministry and I want to advise you. If you keep naming sin, you will never get many meetings and whatever you get will be small." The huge crowds consistently drawn to Van Impe crusades show the fallacy of that advice.

Attempting to tone down Jack Van Impe is like trying to keep a bomb from exploding. Just as John the Baptist thundered against the sins of the Pharisees and Sadducees (Matthew 3:7), and as Jesus blistered his hypocritical hearers (Matthew 23:13-36), so under the power and direction of the Holy Spirit, this fearless evangelist has always laid it on the line.

Even though some pastors trembled a bit when they heard

their church leader's favorite sins named from the pulpit, they rejoiced when hearts began to soften and revival came.

Occasionally, God dealt sternly with the opposition. One preacher rebelled strongly against such plain preaching and attacked the evangelist verbally for his lack of tact. On the second night of the crusade, he had a severe heart attack and Jack continued the meetings without him, still preaching hard against sin. The crusade resulted in a great moving of God in the church.

Most pastors are not petty and troublesome like those just mentioned. Dr. Van Impe has great respect for the pastorate and holds men of God all over the world in high regard. Having worked closely with these dedicated leaders of local churches, he understands something of their burden. He has often been moved by the thoughtless criticism of pastors by people in their congregations.

Once, during a crusade, the minister's wife received a dill pickle with a note stating: "This sour pickle reminds us of you."

The pastor of a small church in California where the Van Impes ministered was living on a weekly salary of fifteen dollars. He and his family, in order to make their income stretch, ate a great amount of macaroni. Critical members grumbled because he didn't provide his family with a more healthy diet.

Unwilling to be a party to such childish sniping at God's servants, Dr. Van Impe has made it a practice to rebuke carnal Christians who gossip in his presence. His sermons, which pound hard at backbiting and slander, have often brought conviction to backslidden, pharisaic, church members who were at the heart of pockets of discontent in congregations. As a result, barriers have been broken down between pastors and people, making revival possible.

Sometimes it is the evangelist who is criticized and opposed.

After an unusual week of blessing in a California crusade, where there were 119 converts and a gracious refreshing in the church, two deacons complained to the pastor because they thought the accordion music had been too loud. Commenting on their attitude, Dr. Van Impe says: "Some believers will gripe in heaven because the streets of gold affect their eyesight."

One young man registered his opposition by getting up during the message and calling the evangelist names.

Sermons in a Pennsylvania crusade were punctuated each night for three nights with a woman screaming angrily at the speaker. She finally had to be carried out by ushers and she continued her hysterical tirade all the way out of the building.

While such experiences were not pleasant, Jack and Rexella remembered that their Lord had foretold difficulties for His servants, saying: "Remember the word that I have said unto you, The servant is not greater than his lord. If they have persecuted me, they will also persecute you; if they have kept my saying, they will keep yours also" (John 15:20).

The years in single church crusades introduced the Van Impes to many new friends. Since the audiences were smaller, they were able to get personally acquainted with a greater percentage of their listeners than is possible in the large united meetings. Many of these people stay in regular contact with them and pray for them.

During that time, it was their practice to stay in the homes of people in the churches were they were ministering. They have many fond memories of good fellowship around tables where they became a part of Christian family circles.

Naturally, over the period of twelve years that they avoided motel accommodations, there were some entertainment experiences that were a bit unusual.

In a Texas church, the pastor had moved just before the crusade, leaving the parsonage empty. The church board, therefore, simply threw a mattress on the floor and told Jack and Rexella to make that their home for their time with them. The temperature was ninety-eight degrees most of the week and there were no screens on the windows. They were nearly eaten alive by bugs. It was a week to remember. Or forget.

One poorly organized pastor hadn't arranged any lodging for them before the crusade and on the first day of the meetings asked for help in housing from the congregation. A visiting couple volunteered their tiny home. They had but one bedroom and so it was necessary for Jack and Rexella to sleep in the kitchen. There they watched from their bed, each morning, as their host and hostess ate breakfast at five o'clock before leaving for work.

When the two travellers finally decided they needed more privacy, there were some who resented their request for motel accommodations. One church cancelled a scheduled crusade because of it. Nevertheless, being confident their decision was in the will of God, they made the policy change. The coming of large united crusades and the heavy load of radio and television work have placed such great demands upon them that few now question their need for a suitable place to be alone while in meetings.

The great variety of personalities and situations encountered in an extensive travelling ministry produce some humorous experiences.

A song leader who loved laughs introduced Rexella, saying: "I know Jack used to be in night clubs. Where did he meet Rexella? In the chorus line?"

When she reached the microphone, Rexella innocently said to the audience: "Don't you listen to him. He was pulling my leg." Though she hadn't intended it as a joke, not thinking of the implications, the crowd went wild with laughter.

At one time Dr. Van Impe weighed sixty pounds more than he does now. He says that he had been under conviction about the problem but that a crusade in Flint, Michigan, underscored his need to lose. When he bent over to pick up his accordion, he heard the frightening sound of ripping cloth. He was standing in front of the choir. Diet and exercise immediately became a way of life.

In an Ohio crusade that started on Tuesday night, many members of the church were absent all during the week. On Saturday, Jack went to the post office to mail a package and found fifteen others waiting at the parcel post window.

As he stepped to one side to look at the line and determine whether or not to wait, a man in front of him growled: "What do you think you're doing?"

Not having intended to cut into the line, Jack answered, "Nothing, sir."

"Don't give me that or I'll push your face in!" the angry postal patron retorted.

The next morning, when Jack turned to look at the choir, the formerly angry man stood before him, now pale with shame. He was a deacon in the church. To his credit, he came to the evangelist with tears and they prayed together. It was a touch of revival, even though it came the hard way for the heart-broken deacon.

Many times in their years on the road, the Van Impes have witnessed the power of God to change difficult situations. Often, in answer to prayer, they have seen serious problems turn into great victories and demonstrations of God's power.

When their records of sermons and music that had been mailed to Hackensack, New Jersey, did not arrive, Jack went to New York City's mammoth post office to look for them. The building is three city blocks long and no one could locate them.

Kneeling there in the post office, Jack asked the Lord to show him where the packages could be found. He then rose and walked about one city block before stopping to ask an employee where he should start looking for them.

"What size are the boxes?" the attendant asked.

Going over to a pile of boxes nearby, Jack replied, "About like these."

In the next moment, realizing he was looking at his own material, he shouted: "Here they are!" When describing the incident, Dr. Van Impe remembers there have been scores of others like it, showing God's faithfulness in answering prayer.

The Saturday night meeting in their Corning, New York, Crusade was postponed because of a blizzard. It seemed such a disappointment because the crowds had been building toward that meeting all week long. The extra meeting, caused by the postponement, was held on Sunday afternoon and resulted in fourteen conversions. Not one of these converted could have attended any evening meeting. All have become faithful workers in that church.

Rev. Ralph Boyer, pastor in York, Pennsylvania, had a wayward son. When the Van Impes held crusades in his church, Jack and the pastor prayed long into the night for the young man, who was at that time an entertainer in night clubs in Atlantic City, New Jersey. The father's tears and prayers made a lasting impression on Jack and he felt confident the son would be saved.

When that miracle happened, he rejoiced with the family. The converted pastor's son is Dave Boyer, who now uses his singing talent for the Lord. The book and film "So Long Joey" are accounts of his life and conversion.

Jack Van Impe's rigid self-discipline and dogged determination have been of great importance in his evangelistic career. He has never missed a meeting, even because of illness. When unable to stand, as a result of back problems for a time, he preached and played his accordion from a chair on the platform. When his clothes and musical equipment were stolen from his car, he ministered in an old pair of trousers left in the locked trunk, and borrowed an accordion. He started his next crusade right on time.

As the word of great crowds and unusual results in Van Impe crusades spread around the nation, Jack and Rexella found invitations for meetings growing beyond their ability to accept them. While at first they had taken crusades in the order of invitation, they now felt an obligation to pray over them and seek the will of God as to where to go first. There was seldom a break between meetings. Often they would close a crusade on Sunday and begin another on Monday or Tuesday, conducting as many as thirty-eight crusades in one year.

They consistently broke attendance records. "Standing room only" crowds became the expected thing. Church buildings became too small. Moving to larger auditoriums to finish crusades became common.

It was evident that a new chapter was about to open in their ministry. There was a tide of blessing running. A feeling of expectancy. Groups of churches were uniting to invite them for area-wide crusades.

Jack Van Impe's uncompromising message and strict adherence to ethical principles had gained him a place of trust among fundamentalists throughout the nation. His Scripture-packed sermons were producing multitudes of genuine conversions. Churches were being revived and helped.

Rexella, the perfect teammate, added a tender touch, and complemented his accomplished accordion work with heart-moving vocal solos and piano specials. All the ingredients were there for a ministry to millions. And God was about to make it happen.

Rexella

CHAPTER FIFTEEN

The Tender Touch

Rexella Shelton grew up in a Christian home and attended the First Baptist Church of Pontiac, Michigan where the well-known Dr. H. H. Savage was the pastor. She had the best of Bible instruction and began singing in church when she was six years old. At twelve, she was baptized. She was active in Sunday School and other church activities and had even influenced some of her friends to come to Christ. No one would have guessed that she was uncertain about her own salvation.

It was after singing in a church service, when she was sixteen, that the moment of truth arrived. Rexella left the service and went to her parents' car, weeping. Following her out to the parking area, her father asked what was wrong.

"Oh, dad," she sobbed, "I've deceived my own heart. I've deceived Dr. Savage, and you, and the whole church. I have known about the Lord all my life, but I don't really know Him."

Resisting the temptation to soothe the feelings of his brokenhearted daughter, Rex Shelton acted wisely. "Be sure, Rexella," he said.

A short time after that, her brother, Bob, led Rexella to Christ.

By the time she met Jack Van Impe at the Youth For Christ Rally in Pontiac, Rexella was spiritually settled. She had attended Bob Jones University and felt the Lord's call to some kind of work in evangelism. She had envisioned a brother-sister team with Bob, but the Lord and a persuasive accordionist changed the make-up of her team.

"I didn't marry 'The Walking Bible,' " Rexella tells young ladies thinking of marriage. "I married a young man who was called into the ministry, whom I loved with all my heart. I respected him and felt we could serve the Lord together."

Rexella says her first year as Mrs. Jack Van Impe was a learning experience. It involved staying in many different homes, travelling to Europe, getting used to being an evangelist's wife, and learning to look at Christ in every circumstance. She speaks of Hebrews 12:2: "Looking unto Jesus . . ." as her verse of that year.

From the start, Rexella and Jack were very much in love. Thrilled with life. They made great plans about their future and an expected family. When the years passed and there were no children, Rexella was disturbed. Her desire to be a mother was strong. She recalls that she identified with Hannah's weeping for a child (I Samuel 1:7-8).

The battle of wills lasted until Rexella was weary of the struggle. Finally she came to the place where she accepted God's will with joy. She laid her desire on the altar. "Whether you give me a family, or not," she prayed, "I rejoice in what my life is going to be, because it will really be the best for me."

Peace came! No children, but contentment. And spiritual children by the thousands have been born through their ministry. Jack and Rexella have a spiritual family that encircles the globe.

After their second year of marriage, Rexella began to see her husband as a man especially blessed of God—one on whom God had placed His hand. Jack was beginning to store much of God's Word in his heart. He was already preaching with such power that her own heart was moved as she listened.

She saw that she had married a very disciplined and determined person and concluded that the path he was following could only lead to good things. Wisely, she encouraged him in his diligence and assisted him with his memorization. She prayed for him often.

Rexella speaking

Today, there are many marriage seminars and an abundance of good books telling how to be a good wife. There were few of these advantages when the Van Impes were newlyweds. Rexella says she learned from the best book of all, the Bible. In addition, she enhanced her education by observing pastors' wives. Most of them were excellent examples. A few were not.

One older pastor's wife gave some of the poorest advice she has ever received. "Keep your husband humble," the lady advised. "Don't be afraid to keep sticking pins in him."

Rexella thought that over and decided it was the wrong way to go. She wisely concluded that a servant of the Lord has enough opposition without having his wife add to the problem by trying to deflate him.

One of the best suggestions Rexella ever received came as she stood beside a casket. She was attending the funeral of a pastor friend's mother. As she stood thinking about the life of the good woman, she was challenged about her responsibility as a Christian wife. At that moment, she felt an arm slip gently around her and heard a message she would never forget. It was an older man speaking: "Mrs. Van Impe," he said, "I just want you to know what a great blessing your husband has been to me. Keep loving him. It will put iron in his spine."

Rexella has followed that good instruction. She speaks warmly of the "love-level" of their relationship, saying they have kept their love young and alive. "I love you" is heard often as they voice their deep feeling for each other. Her statement on love sounds almost like a proverb: "If you have confidence in the love of the person with whom you walk, you can go through fire."

In her ministry of music, this dedicated lady communicates compassion. Her genuine Christian character comes through. She has asked the Lord to make each crusade a new challenge and to keep her spirit fresh. Hundreds of crusade congregations know that her prayers have been answered.

Individuals are her interest. Looking at a large crowd is too impersonal. She ministers to each person in the mass of humanity before her. Her listeners know she cares and they love her for it.

In their early years, Rexella fought the temptation of wanting to be at home more than the evangelistic circuit allowed. She would find herself thinking about how good it would be if Jack was in some other kind of ministry so they didn't have to travel. "You know how good it feels to get home from a vacation," she explains. She longed for a more settled life. An opportunity to live in her own house.

The blessing of the Lord on their work has long since overcome that very human desire. She is caught up in what God is doing and is constantly thankful He has allowed her to be a part of the miracle.

Poor health plagued Mrs. Van Impe for a number of years and undoubtedly contributed to her weariness in travelling. Though it was known to few, she lived with pain for a long period of time and endured three major surgeries. Even then, she missed few crusades. Thankfully, that experience is now past and she enjoys the blessing of feeling well.

Praising God for Rexella's recovery, and moved by the joy she has brought to his life, Dr. Van Impe wrote: "For twenty-four years, my charming wife has travelled with me to many parts of the world in evangelism. Her constant love for Christ has been a real inspiration to me. There have been some dark days when her weakened physical condition indicated that she might be unable to continue her vocal ministry. However, God touched her and new strength has been imparted from His hand.

"Rexella has been called 'kind,' 'gracious,' 'charming,' 'loving,' and 'concerned.' This is because she manifests the fruit of the Spirit. After twenty-four years of marriage, I can say that these terms describe her life."

Recognizing the marked differences in their temperaments and backgrounds, Rexella views their complete compatability as an evidence of God's design. It is true that they are opposites, a common thing for marrieds, but their personalities are complementary. God has used their differences to make them effective. Together, they identify with a wide range of people, a fact that allows them to understand, and to minister to, the needs of many.

Becoming reflective, she shares: "I'm so glad the Great Potter has moulded our lives together and that I have been able to walk with Jack in this great ministry."

Walking with "The Walking Bible" has brought some unique experiences.

One minister approached Rexella claiming to have healing power. She had been ill during the crusade and he wanted to lay his hands on her for healing. Knowing that he rejected the virgin birth of Christ, she rebuked him saying: "According to I John 2:22, you are an antichrist and I don't want to be healed by demonic powers." A strong and courageous statement by one so gentle, but she has the capacity for firmness when it is needed.

Sometimes, those who disagree with her husband's uncompromising stand come to Rexella expressing their opposition. Her quiet nature evidently leads them to believe she will be softer on the issues. They are always disappointed. She is kind, but unmoving. Her compassionate personality does not weaken her convictions.

As might be expected, some unusual experiences have occurred while travelling.

One night, atop a mountain in California, they found themselves in a blinding blizzard. What first appeared as a gentle snowfall became so fierce they were unable to go on. It was bitter cold and there was no help available. All through the night, Jack kept running the engine at brief intervals to keep them from freezing. To make matters worse, the car kept slowly sliding closer to the edge of the mountain. They prayed and waited.

Finally, in the morning, a truck came and they were able to follow him down the mountain.

In the skies over South America, they were in a terrible storm. The plane was tossed about like a toy. Yet, Rexella was able to trust her Lord so completely that she fell asleep on her husband's shoulder.

Talking with Rexella, one quickly detects her great reverence for the man in her life. There is no question that he is the head of their home. Even her choice of clothes is determined by his likes and dislikes. Convinced that he should never have to be concerned about her appearance, she shops to please the Lord *and* Jack, feeling this provides safe guidelines for her ministry to the public. She is also careful not to buy clothing that will draw attention to her person, rather than her message.

Granted, Rexella's attitude is one that is foreign to many in our day, but who can argue with the results? In giving she has gained. A relationship based on mutual love and consideration is unbeatable. Lessons learned here could change the homes of the world.

To see a preacher at a distance is one thing. To see the hand of God upon the man you love is another. Rexella has watched her husband seek the will of God and find it. Never quick to plunge into any project, Dr. Van Impe has been a living example to his wife of one who earnestly communes with God over a matter until he is sure about it. After the decision is made, his great faith has astounded her.

Accepting the responsibility of nation-wide television is a good example. Needing nearly a third of a million dollars to finance the first telecast, he moved ahead, knowing it was the will of God. By the time of airing, the money was there.

Her husband's discernment of the needs of individuals has been a faith builder for Rexella. He boldly confronted one man about the sin of adultery. God had revealed the man's problem to the evangelist on the first night of the crusade. The adulterer was shocked at the revelation. "But how did you know?" he asked. Rexella was amazed at this first demonstration of discernment. Since that time she has witnessed many similar scenes.

On the platform, Rexella Van Impe is a communicator, a channel for God's message in music to millions. Before great crowds, she is herself. At ease, yet controlled. She comes across as the voice of sincerity. But it is deeper than that. So confident is her husband of her sensitivity to the Spirit of God that he often bases his choice of sermon on solos she renders in the meeting. They are a team. His ministry would be weakened without her.

Rexella is a personal worker from afar. She gets close, from a distance. But opportunities come for witnessing to individuals. In Pittsburgh, a college student came to have her Bible autographed. Sensing the young woman had spiritual needs, Rexella asked if she knew the Lord. "No," answered the autograph seeker.

Leaving the crowd gathered around her, she found a quiet place and led the troubled co-ed to Christ. The following night, the new convert handed Rexella a note. It simply said: "Thank you for caring."

A new work for Rexella is that of speaking to ladies' groups during crusades. For a long time she avoided such openings, fearing the people would expect her to be another "Walking Bible." Finally she conquered her apprehensions, and God has blessed her work with women. Nearly one hundred ladies accepted Christ last year in these meetings.

It is difficult to predict the future of Jack Van Impe Crusades. Expansion of outreach is happening so fast that it is impossible to tell where it will lead. But it is certain that whatever develops, the tender touch of Rexella Van Impe will be felt in the total personality of the ministry. And wherever "The Walking Bible" goes, she will be there putting iron in his spine.

CHAPTER SIXTEEN

The Walking Bible

In the minds of millions, Jack Van Impe has become "The Walking Bible." It didn't happen overnight.

Dr. David Allen set the example. His ability to quote the Scriptures in his work as a successful pastor and teacher convinced Jack of the value of memorization. The authority given his ministry by the use of the very words of the Bible was easy to see. It is not surprising that one of his students decided to build on the same foundation.

Jack was not the first Van Impe to be moved to memorize by Dr. Allen. Oscar had also sat through his classes and had been given Scripture memory assignments. The older Van Impe had tackled the project by arranging verses according to Bible doctrines and placing them on index cards that he could carry with him. It was a means of making double use of his time and changed many waiting hours, that would otherwise have been wasted, into profitable opportunities for storing God's Word in his heart.

When Oscar went to Belgium he left his Bible memory cards behind. It was an oversight, but turned out to be a blessed blunder. Jack found them, very near the time of his return from backsliding, and adopted his father's method. He's still using it today.

As a student, Jack found the verses he programmed into his mind were like good friends. They came to his aid when he needed them. Assignments became easier. Witnessing, a

The Walking Bible

natural experience. And, best of all, this army of Bible verses marched into his ordination examination and rescued him from hours of questioning by the ministers present.

When he struggled with the decision concerning the main thrust of his ministry, it was those Bible verses, now leaping into every sermon, that gave him confidence that he was equipped to preach. Without this assurance, it is likely he would have disregarded the disastrous Phil Kerr engagements as anything significant, feeling that music was the only Christian career open to him.

During his evangelistic ministry, the power of God's Word has been consistently demonstrated. He attributes the characteristic lasting effect of his crusades to the saturation of his sermons with the Bible. Sinners are confronted with God's Word, rather than tear-jerking stories. The result is conviction and genuine conversions. Christians are moved to revival because they are forced to see themselves as God sees them. And that is what preaching is all about.

Not everyone appreciates memorization. Even among preachers. One Ohio minister once told Jack that his Scripture quoting was leading him into a stilted form of preaching and would hurt his ministry. Today, the homiletical expert is out of the ministry, after the church died under his polished preaching, while Dr. Van Impe is still quoting Scripture and reaping the benefits of its power.

Since so much of the Bible is prophecy, it was inevitable that one memorizing such a great amount of it would take a special interest in the signs of the times. Being an avid reader and a tireless researcher, Jack saw present-day events fitting perfectly into the prophetic scene. This has been an important factor in the growth of his ministry. He has felt the pulse of his time and as a result has caught the ear of the world. Sermons such as 'The Coming War With Russia," and "Shocking Signs of the End of the Age," have a word for this very hour. And these are not the hysterical speculations of crowd-seeking sensationalism. They are messages packed with Bible proofs. Facts are documented and exposition of the Scriptures is always scholarly and in context.

Having so much of the Bible committed to memory has equipped Dr. Van Impe for encounters with critics and opponents.

Members of cults who have come unsuspectingly to his door have found themselves at a loss to cope with his plain presentation of Bible truths.

Representing the Michigan Sunday School Association in a debate with an atheist and a Roman Catholic priest, on Detroit's radio station, WXYZ, Jack quoted over five hundred Bible verses in the first segment of the program. The moderator was so upset at this domination of the debate with unanswerable arguments that he ruled that no more verses could be quoted in the debate. At that announcement, Jack stated that he would have to leave the program, since the purpose of his being there was to present the Bible. With an hour still remaining in the debate, the announcer rescinded his rule and allowed "The Walking Bible" to keep on quoting Scripture.

The moderator of a radio call-in program in Illinois had Dr. Van Impe for a guest. He hated Christianity and claimed to believe only the Old Testament. When the broadcast started, he announced that, even though this was a call-in show, he would accept no calls from listeners because he wanted to use the entire hour to tear the evangelist to shreds. He started his tirade by saying: "I can't accept the three-headed God of Christians." In other words, he rejected and mocked the Trinity.

"Well, sir," said Jack, "since you believe only the Old Testament, I'll show you what that part of the Bible has to say about the Trinity."

Beginning then at Genesis 1:1 and showing that the very first mention of God is given in the plural Hebrew word "Elohim," he moved through the Old Testament revealing the truth about the Trinity.

He pointed out that the plural word for God (Elohim), was used again at the creation of man (Genesis 1:26), the LORD has a son (Proverbs 30:4), that the LORD speaks to the LORD

(Psalm 110:1), and that the LORD spoke of sending the LORD to the earth (Zechariah 2:10-11).

At that point, the distressed disc jockey decided it was time to open the program to the calls of listeners.

On a network T.V. station in Missouri, Jack debated a college professor. The program started with the announcer telling viewers that the debate was between a fundamentalist and an intellectual. Some put-down! But it didn't matter. After being bombarded with the Bible for twelve minutes, the professor surrendered and Jack had to use the remaining forty-eight minutes of the program giving his testimony.

Some admirers of Dr. Van Impe's ability to quote eight thousand Bible verses, including the entire New Testament, look upon this accomplishment as the result of a divine gift. "Not so," the memory man replies.

Others think he has a photographic mind. "Wrong again," he insists.

What then is the reason for this unusual feat? "Hard work," he replies.

There are three reasons why Jack Van Impe has become "The Walking Bible." They are: desire, discipline, and dedication.

Seeing the benefits of being saturated with the Bible, he wanted them. Enumerating some of the results of such exposure to inspiration, he says: "The Word gives us victory over sin (Psalm 119:11). It makes us clean (John 15:3). It is the source of faith (Romans 10:17). It brings blessing (Revelation 1:3)." (You can tell that he is just beginning to warm to his subject.) He has experienced the difference in his own life. The words of the Bible are no longer just promises for plaques on the wall, nor catchy texts for sermons. They are part and fiber of his very being.

He has demanded the necessary discipline of himself to make his goal attainable. Like Paul, he has mastered his body (I Corinthians 9:27). Depriving himself of relaxation, and sometimes of sleep, he has kept an appointment with the Bible. With his pressing schedule, there have been many times when it would have been easier to forget those two hours of daily memorization. But ease was not his aim. He wanted to be a man of the Word.

Dr. Van Impe says he has spent about eight thousand hours in memorizing eight thousand verses. And that time was all invested for the glory of God. There were no contests to win. No awards to receive. No one challenged him to a memory marathon. His service for Christ here was just as real to him as preaching or leading a soul to salvation. The Scripture memory time was a sacred rendezvous. There were few memory gimmicks used to achieve his goal. The important dimension to this accomplishment was, and is, dedication.

Eager to have others memorize the Bible, Dr. Van Impe has been willing to share the method that has made him "The Walking Bible."

First, he prepares index cards with Bible verses on one side and the references on the other. He generally prepared fifty cards at a time. Others might not want to make that many. The important thing is to get a start with some set number of verses.

He suggests choosing verses by subject or doctrine, not by chapter. At one time, he tried memorizing by chapter, but found himself less able to use the verses quickly. He would lose valuable time working through a number of verses to get to the one he needed. Memorizing by subject, or doctrine, is more liable to bring verses to mind when a given subject is raised.

Use a good concordance (possibly Young's or Strong's), and make a list of choice verses on the particular word or subject you wish to study. For example, you might take the word "save" or "saved" in studying the doctrine of salvation. Placing the verses on your cards chronologically will help to keep your thoughts organized. You may want to use the following verses: Isaiah 45:22, Jeremiah 8:20, Matthew 1:21, Luke 19:10, John 3:17, Acts 4:12, Romans 10:1, I Corinthians 1:21, Ephesians 2:8-9, I Timothy 1:15, 2:4, and Hebrews 7:25.

Memory cards would be as below:

Side 1

Subject: Salvation
Isaiah 45:22

Side 2

"Look unto me, and be ye saved, all
the ends of the earth; for I am God and
there is none else."

Side 1

Subject: Salvation
Jeremiah 8:20

Side 2

"The harvest is past, the summer is
ended, and we are not <u>saved</u>."

Side 1

Subject: Salvation
Matthew 1:21

Side 2

"And she shall bring forth a son,
and thou shalt call his name JESUS; for
he shall <u>save</u> his people from their
sins."

Side 1

Subject: Salvation
Luke 19:10

Side 2

"For the son of man is come to seek
and to <u>save</u> that which was lost."

Side **1**

```
Subject:    Salvation
            John 3:17
```

Side 2

```
    "For God sent not his Son into the
world to condemn the world, but that the
world through him might be saved."
```

Another approach to the choice of verses for memorization, Dr. Van Impe calls: SUBJECT COHERENCE. Here is a sample of that type of study:

1. Sin: Psalm 14:3, 51:5, Ecclesiastes 7:20, Isaiah 53:5 Micah 7:2, Luke 18:19, Romans 3.9-18, 3:23 Galatians 3:22.
2. The results of sin: Ezekiel 18:4, 20, Romans 5:12, 6:23, James 1:15, Revelation 21:8,27, 22:15.
3. The remedy of sin: Isaiah 53:5,6, Matthew 20:28, Romans 5:8, I Corinthians 15:3, II Corinthians 5:21, Galatians 1:4, 3:13, Philippians 2:5-8, I Peter 2:24, 3:18.

A good concordance also provides a means of cross-reference study on two subjects. By memorizing verses on both, a knowledge is gained about how the two relate. A set of verses cross-referencing baptism and salvation might be arranged with comments as helps in the following manner:

1. Why did Christ come? TO SAVE. Matthew 9:13, Luke 19:10, I Timothy 1:15.

2. How did He save? NOT BY BAPTISM: John 4:2, HOW THEN? BY BLOOD: Ephesians 1:7, I John 1:7, Revelation 1:5.
3. What is the Gospel? I Corinthians 15:1-4. TO ADD WATER IS HERESY: Galatians 1:8,9.
4. How can one be saved? THROUGH FAITH—BELIEVING: John 3:14,16,36, 6:47, 8:24, 11:25, 14:1, 20:30,31, Acts 10:43, 13:38, Romans 1:16, 4:3, 4:5, 10:9,10, I Corinthians 1:21, Galatians 2:16, Ephesians 1:13, II Timothy 1:12, II Peter 2:7.
5. Who then should be baptized? THOSE WHO HAVE BEEN SAVED: Acts 2:41, 8:37, 10:47, 16:31-33.

A packet of memory cards on the doctrine of Christ might contain this outline:

1. VERSES ON THE VIRGIN BIRTH OF CHRIST: Isaiah 7:14, Jeremiah 31:22, Matthew 1:23, Luke 1:27, Hebrews 10:5.
2. VERSES ON THE DEITY OF CHRIST: Proverbs 30:4, Isaiah 9:6, Micah 5:2, Matthew 1:23, Acts 7:59,60, Acts 16:31,34, Romans 9:5, I Timothy 3:16, Hebrews 1:8, I John 5:20.
3. VERSES ON THE BLOOD OF CHRIST: Exodus 12:13, Leviticus 17:11, Matthew 26:28, Ephesians 1:7, Colossians 1:13,14, 1:20, Hebrews 10:18, 19, I Peter 1:18,19, I John 1:7, Revelation 1:5, 5:9.
4. VERSES ON THE RESURRECTION OF CHRIST: Matthew 28:6, Mark 16:6, John 2:19, Acts 2:23,24 3:15, 5:30, Romans 1:4, 4:25, 10:9,10, I Corinthians 15:3,4, Philippians 3:10, Colossians 3:1, I Thessalonians 1:10, Hebrews 13:20, Revelation 1:18.

One desiring to be equipped to prove the reliability of the Bible would memorize verses having to do with inspiration. A few might be: Exodus 24:4, II Samuel 23:2, Psalm 119:11, 105, 130, Jeremiah 1:9, 30:2, Matthew 4:4, II Timothy 3:16, II Peter 1:20, 21.

Dr. Van Impe recommends quoting each verse in the first packet aloud, seven times daily for one week. The second week this can be cut to twice each day. The third week once daily will be sufficient.

Meanwhile, a second packet, of perhaps twenty cards, has been added on the second week and the verses are being reviewed seven times daily while going over the first packet twice.

By the fourth week, the original packet will only need to be reviewed one time weekly. That should be continued for three months. After that, a monthly refresher will be sufficient. (All the while each new system is following this pattern.) Finally when a packet of cards is completely mastered, a review once in three months will be enough. Dr. Van Impe now reviews the New Testament every four months.

If all this seems like a lot of work, it should. However, the use of the card packets will allow much of the work to be done in hours that otherwise would have been whiled away in less profitable pastimes. Any time of waiting can be time in the Word.

As has been mentioned, Dr. Van Impe has used few memory aids. Occasionally, he has taken the first letters of a list of names (such as the names of the twelve tribes of Israel) and arranged them into one word. That word, then, no matter how strange sounding, enabled him to remember the entire list. He advises creativity whenever it can be helpful. No amount of memory aids, however, can replace self-discipline. Without that, any memory plan will fail.

The snowballing effect of Dr. Van Impe's memory method is somewhat similar to the results flowing from it in his ministry. Having begun in small single church meetings, this Bible-quoting evangelist now has invitations to hold crusades in some of America's largest cities and in other nations of the world.

Receiving doctorate
L. to R.:
Dr. Hugh Pyle, Dr. Lee Roberson,
Dr. Jack Van Impe,
Dr. Jerry Falwell

CHAPTER SEVENTEEN

Dr. Jack Van Impe

Jack Van Impe started his evangelistic ministry with a crusade in Filion, Michigan, a small town in the state's "thumb" area.

His first large united crusade was in the same vicinity. Eleven denominations took part in sponsoring the meetings and the press gave glowing reports of the public response. The president of the Huron County Evangelistic Association (the sponsoring organization) was quoted as saying:

Two weeks of the most wonderful interdenominational evangelistic meetings Huron County has ever known closed on Sunday night, July 20.

Hundreds listened attentively every night to the forceful, dynamic Bible truth preached by Rev. Jack Van Impe, and to the beautiful hymns sung by his wife, Rexella.

The whole county is stirred, and many who had never thought of doing it before are now leading others to Christ.

Many congregations are reporting their pastors are preaching with a new zeal and real passion for souls. Some are reporting an increase in attendance at their Sunday evening services.

Many have asked forgiveness, and wrongs have been made right. Several pastors have stated that this is the closest thing to old-time revival they have seen.

The write-up for that crusade might well have served as copy for scores of other such united efforts to follow in the years to come. The pattern seemed the same everywhere. Packed auditoriums with overflow crowds, hundreds of decisions, and spiritual refreshment were all a part of nearly every Van Impe area-wide crusade. Of the Jamestown Crusade in New York, Rev. Wayne Hamilton wrote:

> We recently closed an eleven-day crusade in which Rev. Jack Van Impe and his wife, Rexella, The Ambassadors For Christ, of Royal Oak, Michigan served as the evangelistic team.
>
> It is the unanimous testimony of the local Crusade For Christ committee that these were the most successful meetings in the history of our united efforts. We found this couple to be exceptionally talented and dedicated. In all our dealings with them they truly manifested the Spirit of Christ.
>
> Rev. Van Impe has a remarkable command of the Scriptures and builds every message on the Word, quoting chapter and verse proof of the points made. Many testified they had never heard a man preach with greater command of the Bible.
>
> Perhaps the greatest evidence of the work of the Holy Spirit was seen in the fact that literally hundreds of Christians flooded the altar and aisles on two different occasions giving their lives in new dedication to Christ.

The Benton Harbor, Michigan, news story on the Van Impe Crusade carried a familiar message. It described the final service as "the largest crowd ever to assemble for a religious meeting" in that area. That happened again and again in crusades all over America.

With each passing year it became more evident that Jack's decision to make preaching his main ministry was in the will of God. While that move had limited his outreach for a time and had sent him to smaller crowds and more humble surroundings, it had now built him a strong base of friends and prayer warriors who rejoiced in his victories and helped spread the word of the Lord's blessing upon his ministry. With that good gossip going around, he began to receive far more invitations than he could fill; many of them were now coming from large churches and groups of churches for meetings designed to reach an entire area.

Music, though not the major thrust, remained important to Jack and Rexella. They produced a record of accordion music and vocal solos titled "Presenting the Van Impes." Later, they did another titled: "More of the Van Impes." These were forerunners of a wide and useful recording ministry.

A little-noticed, but important, factor in the increasing impact of Jack Van Impe on America's churches must be the intense prayer life of his father. Oscar, now returned from Belgium and carrying on an evangelistic work of his own, was still giving himself to three hours of prayer each day. It will be interesting to discover, someday, how much that constant intercession contributed to his son's success.

Invitations to united crusades kept increasing. By 1968, Jack and Rexella had conducted sixty of them. In May of that year, God moved men to bestow on the evangelist one of the greatest honors of his life. Dr. Lee Roberson, president of Tennessee Temple Schools in Chattanooga, Tennessee, called to inform him that the school wished to confer upon him the degree of Doctor of Divinity.

Dr. Van Impe received his degree on May 27, 1968, after delivering the commencement address to the Tennessee Temple graduates. Others receiving doctorates on that occasion were Dr. Hugh Pyle and Dr. Jerry Falwell.

As might be expected, notes and letters of congratulations came from across the nation as friends sought to convey their feelings to this evangelist who, in their eyes, had earned his degree through long hours of study and faithful service. Jack and Rexella cherish these meaningful messages as heartfelt expressions of Christian love and friendship.

Among them was this significant note from Oscar and Louise. It was both instructive and prophetic:

143

"May God's *POWER*, more than ever, rest upon you! We believe that is the beginning of *greater* things.

"Above all, stick to the *BOOK*! And *God will honour you* as well as men.

Your loving Mother and Father."

In 1976, two more of America's fundamental Christian colleges honored Dr. Van Impe with special recognition. The schools are Baptist University of America, in Decatur, Georgia, and Hyles-Anderson College, in Hammond, Indiana.

At the Baptist University of America, Dr. Elmer Towns, Executive Vice President, announced: "Tonight, the Chair of Evangelism at BUA is being dedicated with the name, Jack Van Impe Chair of Evangelism. Jack Van Impe personifies the aims of Baptist University of America since he stands for the fundamentals of the faith, since he wins the lost through his crusades, since he works with and through fundamental local churches, and since he is an educated, disciplined, and prepared servant."

At the Hyles-Anderson College, Dr. Van Impe was presented a Doctor of Humanities degree. The presentation was made by Dr. Wendell Evans, Chancellor, who stated that Hyles-Anderson College believed that God had raised up Dr. Van Impe to lead fundamentalists—especially in the field of evangelism. Immediately upon the presentation, the entire student body stood and gave Dr. Van Impe a five-minute ovation.

In response to these honors, Dr. Van Impe has said: "Instead of feeling exalted, I am humbled as I realize that so many wonderful Christians love me and depend on me to uphold the banner of Christ and fundamentalism."

144

CHAPTER EIGHTEEN

Crusader

For nearly twenty years, God has been preparing a man. Though the man was not aware of it, the aim of his preparation was a world-wide ministry.

His work had begun in some of the smallest of churches. Accepting that as God's will, he had been faithful over little things. In fulfillment of the biblical promise, he was now to have charge over greater.

Discipline had been an important dimension in his preparation. The Bible says the fruit of the Spirit is "self-control." That truth reveals the reason behind Jack Van Impe's ability to discipline himself for the great task of Bible memorization and excellence in music.

As the direction of his ministry moved toward large churches and united crusades, he was faced with a policy decision formerly unimportant to him. It had to do with the types of churches that would sponsor his crusades. Dr. John R. Rice had been raising this issue in his weekly paper, *The Sword of The Lord,* and he and others were holding meetings on evangelism with Christian leaders across the nation.

At first, Jack considered the whole question unnecessary. Were not souls the deciding factor? Did it make any real difference who put the meeting together? Why should he be concerned about who the local pastors included on their committee? Was a crusade platform so sacred that he must know the

The Van Impes welcomed to the Philippines by Rev. Bob Hughes and crowd

Dr. and Mrs. Van Impe in the Philippines

pedigree of each participant? Could he not trust the Lord to guide the converts into churches where they would grow and mature? These questions dominated his thinking whenever the issue of sponsorship came up.

On the other hand, Dr. John R. Rice had been of immense help to him throughout his ministry. Even those first sermons at Filion had been loaves baked in Rice's oven. Over the years, *The Sword of The Lord* had provided both instruction and inspiration to the young evangelist. He admired Dr. Rice's ability to move men to soul winning, and had caught his vision of mass evangelism from this revered giant of the faith. Now the very man who had been calling for a return to great united crusades throughout the land seemed to be opposing them.

It was a difficult time to be an evangelist. Lines were being drawn. Christian leaders divided. It was a controversy impossible to escape. Everywhere he went for meetings it was the topic of conversation. He was tired of the whole thing and anxious to get on with the business of preaching the gospel.

It was more loyalty than desire that sent Jack to hear Dr. Rice at a meeting on this subject in Chicago. Yet that night was pivotal in his ministry. It is a story in itself. He tells it well:

> During the first twelve years of my ministry I did not understand scriptural separation. One night I attended the great Chicago Convention, where Drs. Bob Jones, Sr. and Jr., Dr. John R. Rice and many other fundamentalists, spoke on the issue of ecumenical evangelism.
>
> Upon hearing these men, I became angry and walked out of the meeting. My embittered nature said, "These men are jealous, bigoted, unloving and unkind." I wrestled with God and His Word. I searched the Scriptures they had presented and discovered that my problem was with God.
>
> Because of that historical meeting, I changed. I have since carried on in the pattern set by Jesus, Peter, Paul and all scriptural evangelists. In 200 mass city-wide crusades, the Biblical standard of sponsorship was upheld. Because of it, the converts were directed into Bible-believing, Bible-

honoring and Bible-preaching churches. Thank God for those who helped me.

Once the conviction was formed it was unmovable. Sure now that this policy on separation was Biblical, he followed it without wavering. To this day, co-operating and sponsoring churches or organizations in a Van Impe Crusade must hold to the fundamentals of the Christian faith.

Evangelist Jack Van Impe took ten years to decide to make the move to a ministry completely given to united crusades. During that time, the momentum toward combined meetings kept increasing. Many of the single church crusades were now held in congregations numbering several thousand members. Those were exciting years.

Two crusades in the great Highland Park Baptist Church in Chattanooga, Tennessee resulted in nearly four hundred conversions. In Syracuse, New York, one thousand came forward at the invitation. The Scranton, Pennsylvania, Crusade resulted in the largest attendance since the days of Billy Sunday.

Taking a break from the regular crusade circuit, the Van Impes made an evangelistic tour of South America. Their friends, Don and Jenny Riggs of Akron, Ohio, accompanied them. Most of the South American meetings were one-night stands, but a longer crusade that ended on a tense note was held in the Panama Canal Zone. The crowds grew so large that it was necessary to move the meetings out of doors. They were in a valley stadium with hills surrounding them. The university had closed the week before due to Communist influence and Jack was preaching on "The Coming War with Russia." Anyone waiting in the hills would have found the evangelist an easy target. He leaned heavily on the Lord and was protected from harm.

Christian leaders began to urge the Van Impes to direct their ministry entirely to large united crusades. Evangelist Robert L. Sumner, a contributing editor of *The Sword of The Lord*,

Autographing

called upon the Christian public to recognize the abilities of the Van Impes in this field. He wrote and published the following article.

Regular readers of *The Sword of The Lord* are probably already familiar with the names of Jack and Rexella Van Impe since there have been so many thrilling reports of their revivals in our "With the Evangelists" column. God has been pleased to bless the ministry of this young couple in a remarkable manner.

While this team has consistently been very popular in single church crusades and has been solidly booked well in advance, it seems that committees planning great, united campaigns should take this young couple into consideration, hence this write-up. God has gifted them with the abilities and talents necessary for such a ministry and the time seems ripe for their launching out in this type endeavor.

So all committees planning united campaigns, it might prove very profitable for you to prayerfully consider this couple. Their convictions are strongly those of the separatist position in both the realm of worldliness of life and of doctrinal apostasy. Both present a personable appearance in dress, deportment, and ministry.

By 1969, the Van Impes had conducted sixty-five united crusades, and the invitations for meetings were coming so fast that there were fifteen hundred churches on their waiting list. There were seven churches in one city requesting meetings.

One of the experiences of that year was rather frightening, but it demonstrated the power and judgment of God. They were conducting a large crusade in New York and one night a liberal minister attended who mocked through the entire message on the cross. Dr. Van Impe warned him from the pulpit that God would deal with such disrespect. A few weeks later, while he was speaking on Sunday morning the church steeple crashed through the roof of his church, landing at his feet. No one was injured, but the city condemned the building and the people did

150

not have the money to rebuild. The event ended the mocker's ministry and closed the church.

In Pontiac, Michigan, Rexella's home, the Van Impe Crusade was held in a large football stadium. On the final night, rain threatened to force the moving of the meeting to a church auditorium, a move that would have reduced capacity drastically. It had rained all day and finally stopped at 7:10 p.m. At 8 p.m. it started to sprinkle. The people prayed and it rained everywhere but in the immediate vicinity of the stadium. Dr. Van Impe remembers: "Everything was drenched except one square block of the city."

An eighty-year-old woman set up their meeting in Spartanburg, South Carolina. When "Ma" Murray wrote them about the crusade the arrangement seemed absurd. But they hadn't reckoned on the ability of this determined lady. She contacted the pastors and contracted for the auditorium. They had the largest crowd ever assembled for a religious meeting in Spartanburg.

At the crusade in Jackson, Michigan, during the summer of 1969, Dr. Van Impe met Rev. Sam Woolcock. He was serving a church there and acted as crusade chairman. One evening after a service, Rev. Phil Anthony, one of the sponsoring pastors, came to Dr. Van Impe and said, "God wants a man to become a city-wide crusader for the fundamentalists. You are the man, and Rev. Woolcock should be your organizational advance man."

The evangelist slept little that night. He had been wrestling with this decision for more than ten years. By morning, he was sure that the Lord had shown His will through the startling statement he had heard the night before. When the Van Impe move to area-wide crusades came, Sam Woolcock became their advance and organizational man. He worked with them for over six years and organized more than 100 large crusades.

Mass evangelism on that scale demanded organization and communication. Dr. Van Impe opened a national office in Royal Oak, Michigan, and in the first issue of his *Newsletter*, in April of 1970, he told about it. He wrote:

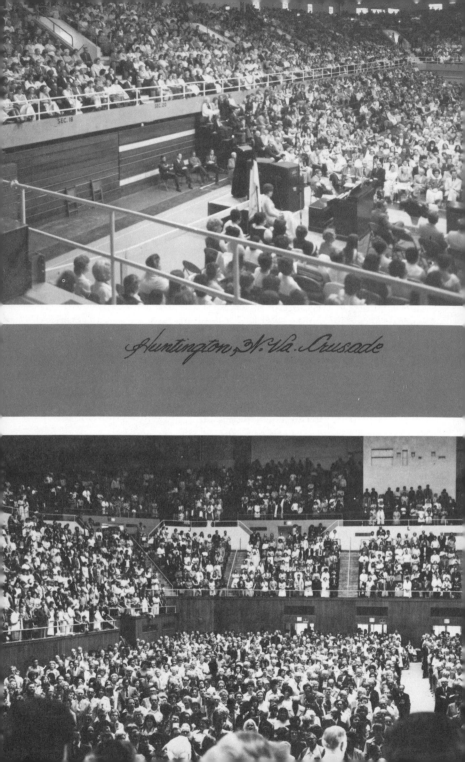

Huntington, W. Va. Crusade

Flint, Michigan Crusade

This is our first news release promised to all of you who voluntarily presented your names in our crusades during the last six months. We want you to know the Lord has certainly been in this decision of going into city-wide crusades full time. Our office is now open. Mr. Frank Lehmann is our executive director and Rev. Sam Woolcock our crusade consultant and organizer. Please place the names of these men on the prayer list along with ours as we need your prayers so desperately.

The infant was born. Though it seemed a giant step to the top at that time, it was only the beginning.

Dr. Jerry Falwell was of immense help to Jack and Rexella in that formative time. He and his church, the Thomas Road Baptist Church of Lynchburg, Virginia, produced and mailed their *Newsletter* for one year at no charge. He urged people to pray for them and to support them. They will always be grateful.

Dr. Falwell's encouragement also launched the recorded sermon ministry. He felt the public needed the message titled "The Coming War with Russia" and urged that it be made available on a record. It was good advice. More than twenty-five hundred people have been converted through that one recorded sermon. Now, a number of Dr. Van Impe's messages are offered on both records and cassettes.

That the nation had been waiting for the Van Impes to bring mass evangelism to its cities is evident by the response to their crusade ministry. America's newspapers told the story. Editorials and news articles still chronicle the impact of the "Crusader" on his land. Their headlines spell out the reactions of reporters to regional revivals:

"Crusade Fills Modern Needs"
"Dr. Van Impe Crusade Draws Young and Old"
"43 Kansas City Area Churches Cooperate in Van Impe Crusade"

Crusader

"War with Russia Inevitable? Yes, Says Evangelist Van Impe"

"200,000 Attend Crusades in 5 Weeks"

In his *Newsletter* of March, 1971, Dr. Van Impe looked backward and forward. Both views were exhilarating:

> 1970 was a great year in the service of our Lord. Over 10,000 made decisions for Christ and thousands more renewed their dedication vows to the Saviour. It was also the year we made the move to go exclusively into city-wide crusades sponsored only by Bible-believing churches. Now as we look to the future it is with real expectation. We have some forty major cities planning great mass crusades.

The "Jack Van Impe Crusades" radio ministry was also introduced in 1971. The first effort was to put the recorded sermon, "The Coming War with Russia," on one hundred stations. By February of 1972, the *Newsletter* announced Dr. Van Impe would go nation-wide with a regular broadcast by April. It was a major step of faith, perhaps unprecedented in religious broadcasting. Uusually there is a gradual build-up of stations over a period of months or years. Here, the entire nation was taken on the same day. Less than one year later, January 7, 1973, the program covered the world. Again, the move was made in one great leap. On that one Sunday, outreach increased from the nation to the world.

The Rev. Chuck Ohman, a longtime friend of the Van Impes, is the announcer for the broadcast. Rexella is the soloist and shares letters with the audience. Dr. Van Impe brings up-to-date crusade reports and a Bible message, often on prophetic subjects.

Besides English, the broadcast is also translated into Russian, Chinese, Spanish, Arabic, and Hebrew. This enables Dr. Van Impe to penetrate areas that are untouchable by conventional missionary means. It is an effective ministry that brings letters from people of many nations who are seeking help and salvation. The program is now heard by listeners to over three hundred stations.

Recordings also reach across national boundaries. In January of this year, Mr. Elmer Klassen of Frankfort, Germany wrote for permission to translate Dr. Van Impe's recording "Hell Without Hell" into written form. Permission was granted, and the finished work—entitled "Where Are You Going When You Die?"—was distributed in Germany, Belgium, Holland, Finland, and Sweden.

The crusades, the heart of the work, have continued to break attendance records and to leave spiritual revival in their wake.

In Indianapolis, twelve thousand gathered for the closing service of the crusade. Hundreds were converted. It was a cold week for outdoor meetings, yet thousands gathered nightly wrapped in blankets to hear "The Walking Bible."

Over ten thousand attended the final night in Dayton, Ohio. It was a week of great spiritual victories with many decisions for Christ.

"Crusade Crowds Larger Than Any Sports Gathering in the History of Hershey, Pa." was the headline on the *Newsletter* reporting that great crusade. The attendance set a record for any religious gathering in that part of the state.

Portsmouth, Virginia, responded so well that closed circuit T.V. was used to accommodate the crowds. There were six hundred conversions.

On September 28, 1973, during their crusade in Lansing, Michigan, a special recognition of their twenty-five years in evangelism was given Dr. and Mrs. Van Impe. At that time it was reported that up to this silver anniversary in soul winning they had seen 125,000 respond to the invitation to receive Christ as personal Saviour, with approximately 500,000 having rededicated their lives to the Lord. Events since then indicate greater things ahead.

While the thrust of the crusade work is on the mainland of the United States, Jack and Rexella took their ministry to Honolulu, Hawaii in 1974. Results there were exceptional. Thousands attended the meetings and there were more than

VAN IMPE CRUSADE
EXCEEDS EXPECTATIONS

RECORDS
TUMBLE !

ATTENDANCE
HITS 10,500

GREATEST
RELIGIOUS
EVENT IN
MEMORY

Hershey, Penn. Crusade

five hundred conversions. Dr. Van Impe appeared on radio with AKU, the highest-paid radio personality in the world and was given the opportunity to answer Bible questions for listeners. Another crusade is planned there soon.

Churches in the Philippines hosted a crusade in January of 1975. One of the high points of this effort was the response of the pastors. Special seminars on soul winning were scheduled for them by Dr. Van Impe, and they resulted in a pledge to try to win ten thousand souls during that year. Decisions for Christ totaled 6,514, making it one of the most fruitful of Dr. Van Impe's evangelistic career.

Jack and Rexella have travelled to the Holy Land on two occasions. Actually walking where Jesus walked has left an indelible impression on them. It has made the Bible message even clearer than before.

Perhaps the most unforgettable experience there was that of ministering in Jerusalem. Fifteen members of the United Nations staff attended that service. Not one of them could understand English, but a missionary translated for them and all fifteen received Christ as personal Saviour. The very purpose of the Lord's coming was fulfilled in their lives.

When you are reaching people with the gospel message, you can expect opposition. Sometimes, real danger.

It was the closing Friday night in their Kansas City Crusade when Dr. Van Impe discovered that his life was in jeopardy. He was announcing the subjects for the final meetings when he saw a dozen policemen enter the building. One of the officers walked to the platform and whispered a message to him. He said, "We have every exit covered because we have received official reports that there is a plot to kill you."

For the next forty-eight hours, the Van Impes were unable to travel without armed guards. Neither hand-shaking nor Bible signing was allowed until the final night of the crusade and even then only with officers present.

Dr. Van Impe remembers that before the police came on the scene, just preceding the service, a man rushed up to him asking for help in the prayer room, immediately. Since there were only four minutes before the service was to start, he told the man he would have to wait until after the meeting. The fellow walked away cursing. Perhaps this was the key move in the planned killing. God knows, and is always on time in protecting His own.

It is known now that three men were involved in the plot. A number of drug pushers had been converted in the crusade and the narcotics traffic had been disrupted. These three decided the troublemaker had to go. Fortunately they did not succeed in their murderous venture. Arriving home safely, Jack and Rexella gave thanks to God for His protection.

Hershey, Pennsylvania, was another danger spot. The crusade crowds were especially responsive with attendance building to 10,500. Revival was in the air. In the midst of this blessing, a note came in the offering that threatened Dr. Van Impe's life if he preached his sermon "A Politician's Greatest Blunder." Masked men attended the meeting on the night of the announced sermon. At the motel where they stayed, the phone rang throughout the night and the calls were not coming through the switchboard, but were being dialed from other rooms. It was a trying time, but once again they were kept from harm.

Dr. Van Impe's most recent deliverance from death came during the Bicentennial Crusade in Philadelphia, held July 4-11, 1976. The experience was explained by the evangelist, himself, in the "Bicentennial/Anniversary Issue" of the *Newsletter*. He reported:

> Praise God, from Whom all blessings flow! God graciously protected the city of Philadelphia, America's 200th birthday celebration, the Bicentennial Crusade, and my life. Instead of violence, blessing occurred the week of July 4 through 11.
>
> The Congressional Record, F.B.I. files, Reader's Digest and the Herald Tribune (international English newspaper), had all carried warnings concerning the planned violence which might have destroyed Philadelphia and the Bicentennial activities. Communists and militant supporters had

mapped out a program in Chicago January 30 through February 1, 1976, to bring "fireworks" to the "City of Brotherly Love" July 4.

In addition to these reports, I had personally received warnings. I was told that militants wanted Dr. Jack Hyles and myself "out of the way."

July 2, Rexella and I left home for Philadelphia. As we stood in the foyer of our home, praying, my heart was heavy. I felt that I might not return. I had said nothing about the mail I had received.

That same morning, my staff had given me a note. It said: "We are praying that God will bring you back to us safely." Every staff member had signed it. Being a man, I fought my emotions, but was deeply moved. I knew God had a plan, and all I wanted was His will.

The evening of July 2 was spent in Philadelphia. Three truckloads of militants arrived in front of our hotel and marched past with the clenched fist salute of the Communist movement. On television, radicals were being interviewed. They boldly boasted of the way they would dynamite the city July 4. I wondered how the T.V. media could be so calloused as to allow these revolutionaries thousands of dollars worth of air time.

The fear could be felt in the air. Millions who had planned to come to Philadelphia stayed away. The downtown hotels were forty to fifty per cent vacant although they had been completely booked months in advance.

On our opening night, fifty of the sponsoring churches believed it best to conduct their own services in order to avoid any violence. Police filled the city, and I was told that the militants were under complete surveillance as plainclothesmen infiltrated their ranks. Six guards were assigned to the crusade platform. My personal bodyguards (one of whom had been personal bodyguard to Mayor Rizzo for three and one-half years) demanded that I wear a bulletproof vest. I tried it the first night and felt handicapped. The next day I said: "Men, I have spent the night in prayer and feel it is a lack of faith to wear this vest for the entire crusade." From that moment onward, perfect peace filled my soul.

Dr. Van Impe's "perfect peace" was from the Lord. Once again, he walked through danger unharmed. It has been said that a man who is in the will of God is perfectly safe until his work is done. And there seems to be a great ministry remaining for this able evangelist.

The outreach of Jack Van Impe Crusades keeps increasing. Crusades, radio, recordings, literature, and now television (viewed this year on over two hundred fifty channels), as well as their missionary work in Belgium, make a mighty load for these servants of Christ. They deserve the prayers of Christians everywhere. And prayer is an important part of their service to others. Dr. Van Impe's father, Oscar, has this special ministry and, along with his work of counselling by mail, intercedes for many troubled people.

In recognition of his work in evangelism, Dr. Van Impe was selected as a speaker for the World Congress of Fundamentalists, which took place June 15-22, 1976 in Edinburgh, Scotland. The honor was extended by Dr. Bob Jones, Jr., Dr. Ian Paisley, Dr. Wayne Van Gelderen, and the World Congress committee. Two thousand delegates, representing every continent, attended. Dr. Van Impe presented a paper on "The Fundamentalist and Evangelism."

Even an evangelist needs a pastor. In recent years, two men have capably filled that need. Rev. Robert Shelton, Rexella's brother, followed Dr. Savage as pastor of the First Baptist Church of Pontiac, Michigan, and was the Van Impes' minister for a long period of time. He is now in Bible conference and evangelistic work.

Later, Dr. G. B. Vick of Temple Baptist Church in Detroit became their pastor. His ministry and help greatly blessed both Jack and Rexella. Dr. Vick was deeply committed to the Van Impe evangelistic team and since his death has been sorely missed.

Many dedicated people are involved in making the present

ministry of Jack Van Impe Crusades possible. It is a large work, having taken them to more than two hundred united crusades. Research indicates this to be the most extensive effort in mass evangelism in this century, apart from Dr. Billy Graham.

This has called for an increased staff; there are more than forty employees in this growing organization. Mr. Greg Harrell, a man devoted to the Lord and to Dr. Van Impe, is the capable executive director of the work. In addition to the leadership given by the Van Impes, guidance is given to the ministry by a capable board of directors. At this writing, men on that board are: Attorney, Chris Powell (chairman); Mr. Ralph Hamlin; Dr. T. Dwaine McCallon; Rev. Charles Ohman; Rev. Robert Shelton; Mr. Albert F. Young; Mr. Jon Byrd; Rexella, and Dr. Van Impe (president).

While other vehicles of outreach minister to millions, it is likely that mass evangelism will continue to be most important to Jack Van Impe Crusades.

CHAPTER NINETEEN

More Important Than Money

John Wesley feared the tyranny of money so much that when he became rich through the sale of his books, he gave all his wealth away. Jack and Rexella Van Impe saw a similar problem approaching and headed it off by arranging for all of their income to support their world radio outreach. Had they not taken precaution, they would now be millionaires. That is not their goal.

Knowing that many great ministries have been ruined by greed and bad financial policies, Dr. Van Impe has built safeguards into his organization so that Christian people can be sure their gifts will be used wisely in Christ's service.

"How much did you make on your national telecast?" he was asked on a Pennsylvania T.V. program.

"Nothing," he answered. "I lost $235,000. And I invite you to come to our headquarters and examine the books. I have nothing to hide." It was no bluff.

The emcee would have been welcome in Clawson, Michigan, at the international offices. Investigating, he would have found that the telecast was only possible through gifts by churches and individuals who were interested enough in carrying the gospel to the nation to support the telecast. Viewers contributed only a fraction of the cost.

The financial need to sustain the world ministry of Jack Van Impe Crusades is staggering. Costs for radio and television time, records, literature, cassettes, personnel, crusades, and other areas of outreach are expected to top two million dollars this year. Most of the income arrives in small amounts by mail. To be sure he is never affected by the sight of money coming in, Dr. Van Impe avoids opening crusade correspondence. Six secretaries open all letters and channel the money to its proper place before he views the personal messages directed to him.

The salary arrangement for Dr. Van Impe is unique; it is all paid by his board members. Every donated dollar finds its way into the work, providing a great investment opportunity for those eager to get the most mileage out of their giving.

His strong Biblical stand and sound financial policies have gained Dr. Van Impe the respect and support of many Christian leaders. The following comments by a number of these stalwarts of the faith came as a result of my request, as his biographer, for some statement about him and his ministry.

Dr. Joseph M. Stowell, D.D. (National Representative of The General Association of Regular Baptist Churches): "I have known Jack Van Impe for a number of years and have been privileged to work with him in evangelistic campaigns. He is true to the Bible, has a burning zeal for the lost, and is fearless in his presentation of divine truth. He sees the issue of the apostasy and is obedient to the Bible teaching concerning separation from it. He not only believes in and preaches ecclesiastical separation, but he believes in and practices personal separation. He and his wife, Rexella, have made a wonderful team."

David Otis Fuller, D.D.: "I have known Jack and Rexella for a number of years and both Mrs. Fuller and I think in highest terms of them. We had them for two campaigns in Wealthy St. Church (Grand Rapids, Michigan) when I was still pastor. The last night of one of those campaigns, with closed circuit TV, we had the largest crowd that church ever held, some twenty-four hundred".

Dr. David Cavin (Pastor of High Street Baptist Church, Springfield, Missouri): "Dr. Jack Van Impe in his Bible-centered ministry has come to the attention of Christians

Rev. and
Esther Shelton,
Rexella's parents

Oscar and Louise
Van Impe

Dr. and Mrs. Van Impe

everywhere. His ministry is most dynamic, Christ-exalting, and Bible-centered. He has on numerous occasions preached for me, each time to the delight of our church and our city. I am glad to add my testimony on his ministerial blessing to me personally. Rexella Van Impe has with her touch of Christian femininity added a sweetness that God has certainly blessed."

Dr. Lee Roberson (Pastor of Highland Park Baptist Church, Chattanooga, Tennessee and President of Tennessee Temple Schools): "Dr. Van Impe has conducted a number of successful revivals in our church. In the course of these meetings hundreds have been saved and even thousands have responded to the invitation for salvation and dedication of life. He has been a favorite at the Highland Park Baptist Church and Tennessee Temple Schools through the years."

Dr. John R. Rice (Editor of *The Sword of The Lord*): "Dr. Jack Van Impe is a good friend. He is a fine gospel preacher. He is separated and stands true, does not have any fellowship with modernists and unbelievers, but in his campaign enlists those who are of like precious faith who hold to the great essentials of the faith. God bless him."

Dr. Jerry Falwell (Pastor of Thomas Road Baptist Church, Lynchburg, Virginia): "Dr. Jack Van Impe has conducted several highly successful crusades in the Thomas Road Baptist Church. I consider Dr. Van Impe one of the most dynamic and powerful Bible preachers in the land today. My wife and I are happy to own Jack and Rexella as dear and personal friends.

"More than anyone else on the scene in this generation, Dr. Jack Van Impe has awakened a great interest in prophecy in the hearts of God's people. He has alerted the Christian public to the lateness of the hour and the critical state of the world as it relates to freedom and the scourge of Communism. He has used this information as a challenge to souls to turn to Christ.

"Dr. Van Impe also has the distinction of being the only preacher in this generation who has been able to rally the fundamentalist churches into successful co-operative evangelism. At his young age it is obvious to me that his greater ministry is yet future."

Dr. Jack Hyles (Pastor of First Baptist Church of Hammond, Indiana): "Dr. Jack Van Impe has been the answer to the prayers of thousands of fundamentalist people across America. His message has been clear; his convictions have been firm; his zeal has been a pattern and his love for Christ, for souls and for the brethren has never wavered in the years I have followed his ministry. Many of us have prayed for an evangelist who in every sense of the word is a fundamentalist, and is happy and not ashamed to bear the stigma involved. Here is a man who has sacrificed for his convictions and who has been honored for it. America had to have him. I am pleased God has given him to us."

Dr. Robert Sumner (Evangelist, and editor of *The Biblical Evangelist*): "We consider Dr. Van Impe one of the finest evangelists in our day, certainly the one whom God is using in the greatest outward manner in Biblically-oriented united evangelistic crusades. Other few men have bigger crowds, but they do it at the expense of violating Biblical principles. Dr. Van Impe, who saturates his sermons with the Word of God, refuses any and all entangling ties with apostasy in his meetings. In fact, he speaks out boldly and strongly against modernism, worldliness, false cults and other evils of the day."

Evangelist Fred. M. Barlow, D.D. (Sunday School Consultant, Regular Baptist Press): "When I hear the name Jack Van Impe, I think of Christ's parable of the talents recorded in Matthew 25:14-30. I am well aware the talents of that text were money—mercenary means that the stewards of their lord were expected to multiply through industrious, intelligent, dedicated service for their master. One was given five talents, two to another, and one to a third man.

"In this profile my comparison of Jack Van Impe to that

parable is not in the financial but in the spiritual usage of the term talent. For that is what Van Impe is—talented, tremendously talented!

"Consider a case in point: Jack Van Impe is considered one of the five foremost virtuosos of the accordion in the world, and he is acclaimed as 'master' of the modern invention, the accorgan, 'a transistorized instrument which combines the amplified accordion with electronic organ, harp, bells, chimes, electric piano, banjo, and even marimba and concert string bass with a total of nearly thirty instrument sounds.'

"Combining his musical mastery with the piano artistry and soprano stylings of his wife, Rexella, the Van Impes produce a musical program in their campaigns that is so talent-laden, one religious writer witnessed, 'The musical program alone is so fantastic it would surely pack any auditorium where the Van Impes are appearing.'

"But music is only one of Van Impe's many talents. Consider his mastery of the Bible. Often called the 'Walking Bible,' Jack has committed to memory over 8,000 Bible verses, the 'equivalent of the New Testament.' Suffice it to say, his sermons are Scripture-saturated and, as such, are messages pulsating with divine power; messages that probe, penetrate the hearer's heart; messages that possess authority that comes from God honoring His word; messages that persuade and provoke decisions."

T. Dwaine McCallon, M.D., F.A.A.P. (Jack Van Impe Crusades board member): "Brother Campbell, to ask me to offer a comment on Jack's work is akin to ringing up heaven and asking Barnabas to look back in retrospect and comment on the possible effectiveness of his friend Paul's ministry. I proudly confess my lack of objectivity in evaluating the effect of the Van Impe ministry. I've known in my deepest prayers that this man is one of God's greatest channels of last warning to the world before our rapture. I've stood dumb-struck in his office as six or eight or ten occurrences take place in front of our eyes over a few days in order to open a new path God has directed in Jack's ministry. I've seen the hand of God open doors, change real estate, provide media openings where only brick walls had been apparent.

"I have never encountered a man with the intellectual capacity for understanding and assimilating new facts into an overall cohesive understanding as does Jack Van Impe. The amazing couplet of genius in his mind is completed by his concentration and drive when he undertakes a study of God's Word. This combination of dedicated work and purpose carries forth from his study into the sermon, into the city coliseum and to the airwaves of the world. When yielded to the guidance of the Holy Spirit, Jack has no thought of personal danger, embarrassment of the devil's crowd or lack of boldness in shouting forth God's message of the hour.

"This total immersion of his effort into God's Word is the key to this ministry's success. The Word is still the 'two-edged sword' —praise God we have a swordsman with the stature to firmly take its grip and swing fearlessly through the present deception about us!

"Unknown to the public but shared by you and me is Jack's tenderness and burden of tears for the lost. I could go on about the quality of this man, about his total honesty of word and deed, about his refusal to take even adequate salary until his board insisted, about his hours in the valley when pierced to the core by the malicious acts of others toward him, about his forgiving spirit and unwillingness to believe Christians would allow Satan to use them to attack him and his work and on and on . . ."

Needless to say, space has not allowed the full text of these commendations. But the message comes through. Here is a man who has chosen God instead of mammon. Principles instead of popularity. And his Lord has honored him for it.

If you were to ask Dr. Van Impe why he has taken this route in life, you might well be answered with the words of Solomon: "A GOOD name is rather to be chosen than great riches, and loving favor rather than silver and gold" (Proverbs 22:1).

Dr. and Mrs. Van Impe

CHAPTER TWENTY

To God Be The Glory

Jack Van Impe, saved out of night clubs and beer gardens, has been given a ministry to the world. And as Spurgeon might have said: "It has been all of grace."

There seems little doubt about the success potential of this accomplished musician had he not been converted and called into the work of Christ. It is likely that he would have spent his life reaching ever higher in the entertainment world, only, at the end of the show, to find he had missed the best in life. A frightening thought. And, thankfully, one that needs not be entertained. In giving his life to Christ, he has been blessed beyond all his expectations.

It has been said that Dr. Van Impe is especially gifted. But even that fact should glorify the giver: "A man can receive nothing, except it be given him from heaven" (John 3:27). And the more gifted the man, the greater his responsibility: "For unto whomsoever much is given, of him shall be much required" (Luke 12:48).

Responsibility is a dimension of this story that must not be missed. The crowds, the television appearances, and the articles so well-worded by the press, sometimes give the impression that the work of a man who has the ear of his age is all glamour. Few understand the burden of ministering to the world.

Almost overwhelmed by the charge given him, Dr. Van Impe prepared an article for his *"Newsletter"* titled: "The World is

My Parish." In this communication to his friends, he bares his heart.

Let him tell it:

"John Wesley, the founder of Methodism often said: 'The world is my parish.' He undoubtedly based this statement upon the words of our Saviour who said in Mark 16:15: 'Go ye into all the world, and preach the gospel to every creature.' This past week I realized, as never before, the truth of Wesley's quotation in my own life.

"My staff gave me a bundle of mail from scores of nations. As I read the letters, I began weeping because I realized for the first time how hungry hearts, world-wide, were expecting me to be their pastor, shepherd, minister and guide. As the realization of this truth gripped me I bowed my head and prayed: 'Dear Heavenly Father, I see in a new way the tremendous responsibility that you have placed upon me. Multitudes are depending upon the words that I give them each week to satisfy their spiritual hunger. I will pray harder than ever and study Thy Word ceaselessly so that my ministry may benefit these precious souls in a greater way. Accept the re-dedication of my life and ministry this day because I ask it in the name of the Lord Jesus Christ.'

"This burden was generated when I started to read and organize the letters in an orderly fashion for this issue of the paper. I have become a minister to tens of thousands and perhaps millions in America, Russia, China, Africa, the nations of Europe, and South America.

"Beloved, truly the world has become my parish and I am so humbled by this gigantic undertaking that I can honestly say that much weeping has taken place this day as I re-read the letters over a number of times. I praise the Lord for His goodness in allowing an insignificant person such as I am to be entrusted with this Holy calling."

And what about the future? If the past few years are an indication of things ahead, the load this man of God carries will increase. Still, his burden for souls drives him on. He talks of a larger television ministry, expansion of his literature work, possibly a film outreach, and as you listen you know his heart is open to any new challenge that will honor his Lord.

Given his present grueling schedule, and his demand for perfection, one wonders how much more responsibility could be added. Paul's question to Corinthian Christians seems in order: "And who is sufficient for these things?" (II Corinthians 2:16).

But the pattern of the past charts greater things to come. New doors seem sure to open for the man they call "The Walking Bible." His answer to those who caution him as to his limit is likely to be similar to Paul's: "Not that we are sufficient of ourselves to think anything as of ourselves, but our sufficiency is of God" (II Corinthians 3:5).

Higher hands have guided this Bible-quoting evangelist in the development of his ministry to the world. He and his team have shared in many miracles. They know this work is of God and its expansion around the world is due to the power of His Word. Its future is secure in Him.

To God be the glory!

Index of Persons Other Than Van Impes